Praise for
Secrets of Successful Telephone Selling

"From getting past the discomfort of cold calling to moving past gate-keepers to closing the sale, Bob Bly is there holding our hands all the way. His new book is truly a *complete* guide to telephone selling. I recommend it highly to anyone who wants to use the telephone for sales. I've been selling on the telephone for almost 35 years and I still learned a great deal from Bob's book."
—Joyce L. Gioia, MBA, CMC, consultant and professional speaker

"Bob Bly's new book is a treasure of strategies, techniques, and contacts that can double your closing rates. It is required reading for anyone who wants to take a quantum leap in success. Bob provides a complete road map to achieving your telephone sales goals."
—Paul Karasik, author of *Sweet Persuasion* and *How to Make It Big in the Seminar Business*, founder, American Seminar Leaders Association

"Telephone selling may be the cost-effective method of marketing. Bob Bly's new book is a practical easy-to-read and thorough primer on all aspects of telephone marketing."
—Neil Raphel, Raphel Marketing, Inc.

"Every page of this book is filled to overflowing with great ideas. Having been in sales all of my life, I know a great book when I read it. Bob Bly has done it again. If obtaining leads, closing sales, creating repeat business, and getting referrals are what your business needs (and whose does not?), you will find as I did that this book is exactly right."
—Dottie Walters, president, Walters International Speakers Bureau, publisher/editor of *Sharing Ideas Magazine*

Secrets of
Successful
Telephone Selling

Also by Robert W. Bly

Targeted Public Relations

Selling Your Services

The Copywriter's Handbook

Secrets of a Freelance Writer

Business-to-Business Direct Marketing

The Elements of Business Writing

The Elements of Technical Writing

The Advertising Manager's Handbook

How to Promote Your Own Business

Ads That Sell

Creative Careers

Dream Jobs

Create the Perfect Sales Piece

Keeping Clients Satisfied

Secrets of
Successful
Telephone Selling

How to Generate More Leads,
Sales, Repeat Business, and
Referrals by Phone

Robert W. Bly

AN OWL BOOK
Henry Holt and Company
New York

Henry Holt and Company, Inc.
Publishers since 1866
115 West 18th Street
New York, New York 10011

Henry Holt® is a registered
trademark of Henry Holt and Company, Inc.

LIBRARY OF CONGRESS CATALOGING-IN-PUBLICATION DATA
Bly, Robert W.
Secrets of successful telephone selling: how to generate more leads, sales,
repeat business, and referrals by phone / Robert W. Bly.—1st owl book ed.
          p.   cm.
          "Owl book."
          Includes index.
          1. Telephone selling.   I. Title.
HF5438.3.B58   1997   96-40389
          658.8'4—dc21   CIP

ISBN 0-8050-4098-6

Henry Holt books are available for
special promotions and premiums.
For details contact:
Director, Special Markets.

First Edition—1997

Designed by Kathryn Parise

Printed in the United States of America
All first editions are printed on acid-free paper. ∞

10 9 8 7 6 5 4 3 2 1

Portions of chapter 9, "Getting Past the Secretary," are reprinted, with permission, from the book *Selling Your Services* by Robert W. Bly (New York: Henry Holt & Co., 1991).

Chapter 10, "Follow-up," is reprinted, with permission, from the October 1995 issue of the newsletter *The Art of Self-Promotion* by Ilise Benun (Hoboken, N.J.: Creative Marketing and Management).

Portions of chapter 12, "Customer Service," appeared in a slightly different format in the book *Keeping Clients Satisfied* by Robert W. Bly (Prentice Hall, 1993). Reprinted with permission.

To Ilise Benun—
a master of the soft sell

☎ *Contents* ☎

Acknowledgments   xi

Preface   xiii

A Note on the Terminology   xv

One: Increasing Your Profits with Teleselling   1

Two: The Elements of Successful Telephone Selling   20

Three: Creating an Effective Telephone Selling Center   40

Four: Creating a Telephone Selling Plan That Works   54

Five: Where to Find Good Calling Lists   62

Six: Cold Calls: The Opening Script   76

Seven: Cold Calls: The Presentation Script   85

Eight: Cold Calls: The Objection Script   97

Nine: Getting Past the Secretary:
        The Challenge of Selling to Businesses   113

Contents

Ten: Follow-up   121

Eleven: Closing the Sale   142

Twelve: Customer Service:
          Improving Teleselling Results   155

Thirteen: Add-on Sales   178

Fourteen: The 17 Most Common Telephone Selling
            Mistakes and How to Avoid Them   187

Index   211

Acknowledgments

Selling is a skill area in which you never stop learning. As has been said many times by many people, "School is never out for the professional." And so I want to thank those teachers who have contributed to my sales education: Ilise Benun, Gary Blake, Jim Day, John Finn, Cameron Foote, John Friedberg, Rob Gilbert, Madison Gross, Bob Jurick, Paul Karasik, Jeffrey Lant, Dr. Andrew Linick, Ken Paston, Howard Shenson, Pete Silver, Steve Tayback, Dottie Walters, Fred Weiss, and Mary Anne Weinstein.

Thanks as always to my agent, Bonita Nelson, and my editor, Cynthia Vartan. Helping businesspeople by writing books is one of my great passions in life. Without these two professionals, my opportunities to do so would be fewer and farther between.

I'd also like to thank my clients. Most of what I know is a direct result of working with you. Every day I learn something new from your experience and wisdom.

☎ *Preface* ☎

The business world today is tougher and more competitive than ever. Customers are more demanding, the competition is more aggressive, and traditional selling and marketing methods may not be working as well as they once did. Businesspeople are looking for answers, searching for new and better ways to build sales, make more money, and retain valued customers.

Ironically, the instrument that can dramatically increase your company's sales and profits is sitting, largely untapped, right on your desk: It's your telephone.

The telephone can supplement, augment, enhance—and in certain cases, even replace—print advertising, direct mail, Yellow Pages, on-the-road sales reps, trade shows, and other traditional means of marketing and selling that have become too expensive or too ineffectual.

The problem is that many businesspeople don't know how to effectively use the telephone as a prospecting, selling, closing, and customer-service tool. Nor do they understand how to integrate telephone selling with on-the-road sales reps, direct mail, and other sales and marketing activities.

Preface

Secrets of Successful Telephone Selling presents solutions to these problems. It provides a step-by-step program with easy-to-follow guidelines and sample dialogues telling you exactly what to say, to whom, and when. You learn how to use the phone to generate leads, qualify prospects, follow up on inquiries, close sales, service accounts, get repeat orders, and generate profitable referrals. A businessperson possessed of this knowledge will have a reliable tool he or she can use to generate as much sales volume as desired, and need never fear slow times again.

Virtually everybody in business today sells over the phone at least part of the time. This book is written to help you do it more effectively, with greater confidence, comfort, enjoyment, pride—and results.

A Note on the Terminology

Many people use the terms "telemarketing" and "teleselling" interchangeably, although they in fact mean different things.

Telemarketing is "marketing conducted via the telephone." The aspect of marketing that telemarketing deals with is promotion: The telephone is used to promote products and services. Promotions are a form of mass communication—a single offer, or "pitch," aimed at multiple prospects—which is why most telemarketing calls are scripted and why most telemarketers are not permitted to stray significantly from the script.

Teleselling is "selling conducted via the telephone." Selling involves one party's convincing another party to buy the first party's product or service. The essence of selling is one-on-one persuasion and negotiation, and the essence of teleselling is one-on-one persuasion and negotiation over the phone, where the telephone sales representative is given fairly free reign in what he or she can say and do to close the deal. Teleselling is an individual communication, personalized to each prospect and each situation.

Secrets of *Successful* Telephone Selling

☎ *One* ☎

Increasing Your Profits with Teleselling

I rent space in an office building occupied primarily by small businesses. There is an accountant, a property management firm, a TV repair service, a fish wholesaler, an ambulance service, a financial planner, a therapist, a collection agency, a landscaping company, and me, the trainer, consultant, and writer.

When you're in a small office building, you see your neighbors going in and out, or picking up their mail, and you talk with them. Most of the time it's just "Hello" and "How's it going?" But sometimes the discussion becomes more substantial. Usually this means we end up chatting about the economy in general, and the state of business in particular.

And it's a funny thing: Whether I'm talking with the accountant, the fish seller, or the landscaper, when the discussion turns to business or the economy, the response I get is usually the same: "I'm not enjoying myself anymore. Business is much tougher today than it was ten or fifteen years ago. Customers are fussier, more particular, and more sophisticated. They know what they want, and they demand you give it to them. Making the sale takes longer. And to keep your buyers happy, you must provide an extraordinary degree of customer service."

The recession was the start of tough times for business. And there's no end in sight. Today there's more competition than ever. It has become a buyer's market instead of the seller's market that existed when I opened my business years ago. Customers are extremely price-conscious and have smaller budgets.

People are pressed for time. This makes them impatient. We live in the nanosecond nineties—the Age of Now. Customers want everything done yesterday. If you can't accommodate them, they'll go somewhere else.

You can still succeed in business today. You can make a good living. But not as easily as in the 1970s and 1980s. Prices and fees are down; commissions, salaries, and budgets are frozen. Most people I know are working harder and longer. They are afraid of losing customers; afraid of getting fired; afraid that if they take their two weeks' vacation they won't have a job when they get back. Many of my corporate clients are at their desks early in the morning and late into the night.

This new marketplace, in which fear permeates and the customer dominates, has put pressure on businesses to get more customers and make more sales, to make up for shrinking profit margins and vanishing customer loyalty. The ability to gain new customers—and get more orders from existing accounts—is crucial to survival. But are conventional sales and marketing techniques doing the job?

OF CONVENTIONAL MARKETING AND SELLING TOOLS: REASONS FOR THE DECLINE IN PERFORMANCE

Conversations with executives and entrepreneurs reveal a decline in performance of, and increasing lack of confidence in, traditional sales and marketing vehicles. I frequently hear comments like these:

"Ads are more expensive than ever. But with so much to read, and so many advertisers, our ad gets lost in the publication. We don't know if anyone is reading our ads or what effect the ads have on sales. Inquiries, when generated, rarely result in a sale. My feeling is that the ads don't pay for themselves. We do it mainly to build 'image.' But does that increase sales? I can't tell."

"Trade shows are an enormous drain on our marketing budget. We're in the major shows primarily because our absence would be noticeable, and people might talk if we were *not* there. But it's difficult to directly attribute any new sales or accounts to our trade-show program. Going to shows costs too much and takes up too much time, especially given the recent downsizing of our staff."

"Direct mail is less effective than it was a decade ago. Our responses are way down. And those who do respond either don't buy or take an enormously long time to close. Sending out a mailing to generate leads doesn't work well anymore, unless we aggressively follow up with phone calls."

"Our main source of business has been the Yellow Pages. But ads are getting more expensive. We can't compete with bigger companies running half-page and full-page ads. Our small ad gets lost. We pay more each year and get fewer calls. The Yellow Pages eats up a bigger and bigger chunk of our marketing budget each year. It's becoming unaffordable."

"We've begun promoting our products on the World Wide Web. But I get the sinking feeling that the only people making money on the Internet are those promoting seminars titled 'How to Make Money on the Internet.' The inquiries we get from our on-line postings and home page are mainly garbage. The Internet is filled with many browsers but few buyers."

"Having salespeople on the road is how we traditionally generate business. But the cost is skyrocketing out of control. Also, prospects are busier than ever, so they have less time to see our salespeople. It's harder to get in the door. And you have much less time to make your pitch."

"We still make money mailing our catalog to our customers. But with rising printing, postage, and list-rental costs, we are losing money when we mail it to rented lists. How will we get new customers in the future?"

Do these circumstances mean that traditional marketing and sales tools have been rendered wholly ineffective? Not at all. Many businesses are still getting good results. The problem is, the traditional methods no longer generate the volume of business most of us need to survive and prosper.

The selling effort must intensify. You must get in front of prospects, gain their attention, make your case, and then follow up relentlessly until the sale is made. Most businesses have many potential customers, but they are scattered throughout their city, state, the country, or the globe—more people and locations than they can economically send salespeople to visit.

The solution? A sales tool that combines the economy of mass promotion with the personalized approach of one-on-one, face-to-face selling: the telephone.

Of course, telephone selling is not new. Manufacturers, business professionals, service firms, financial institutions, direct marketers, tradespeople, and business-to-business marketers have been using the telephone as a sales tool for decades. According to Robert Warde, a managing editor at Kipen Publishing Corporation, approximately 800 million calls per day are made in the United States from 155 million telephones. An article in *Starting Smart* newsletter reports that each working day, more than a hundred thousand salespeople place over a million sales and customer-service telephone calls.

Is it time for you to reevaluate how you use the telephone and where it fits into your sales and marketing mix? Today you need sales and marketing methods that are results-oriented and generate rapid revenue. The telephone is such a tool. Here are just some of its advantages over other sales and marketing vehicles.

Ten Key Advantages of Using the Telephone as a Sales Tool

1. The Telephone Can Be Extremely Effective.

Sales trainer Paul Karasik says, "You pick up the phone, you dial the numbers, you make the sales." The telephone is a results-oriented medium. It is not aimed at building image, creating brand awareness, or promoting your reputation. The purpose is to generate an immediate sales lead, qualify a prospect, set up an appointment, or make a sale.

Use of the telephone as a sales tool is growing. According to an article in *Selling* magazine, IBM expects as many as 80 percent of all worldwide sales transactions to be handled by phone. In today's busy world, a telephone call is often the only way to break through the clutter and grab the attention of the businessperson or consumer.

The telephone often works well—but not always. No sales or marketing method generates spectacular results 100 percent of the time. But today, the telephone seems to work more frequently and effectively than many other sales and marketing methods.

"But people hate getting sales calls," you protest. Maybe so.

But have you ever gotten a sales call that interested you because the caller was offering something of immediate concern and relevance to you?

This is, in essence, the secret of successful telephone selling: Do not try to push junk on people who don't want or need it. Instead, call the right people with the right offer—something that solves a problem they have, fills a need, or delivers a result or benefit they want. When you have something that is important to the prospect, people will stop and listen. When you are just "telemarketing"—pushing unwanted merchandise on uninterested people—they won't.

2. *With the Telephone You Get Relatively High Response Rates.*

Response rates to telephone sales calls will vary widely, depending on the market, the product or service, and your goal—whether you are generating a lead, arranging a meeting, or making a sale. As a rule of thumb, response rates for cold calls to a prospect list can range from 5 to 50 percent. They can be lower. They are rarely higher.

A 5 percent response rate means that for every 20 calls you make, you will get one positive response. That's not bad. After all, how long does it take to make 20 phone calls? The 5–50 percent response rate to telephone sales calls compares favorably with direct mail, which typically generates response rates of 0.5 to 2 percent, or with print advertising, where less than 0.1 (a tenth) percent of the readers of a particular newspaper or magazine will reply to your ad.

A telephone response of less than 5 percent is not necessarily a bad thing. If you sell high-priced products and services, you may be able to achieve your sales goal for the week with just one or two orders. The higher the price, the lower the response rate you need to make a profit.

At the same time, you want to constantly refine your approach to see if you can increase response. The better your response rate, the greater your sales.

With a higher response rate, you have to make fewer calls to achieve your sales goal, so you can spend less time selling each day. With a 1 percent response rate, you must make 100 telephone calls to generate one positive response. With a 10 percent response rate, getting that positive response requires only ten calls.

3. The Telephone Cuts through the "Paper Glut" in the Prospect's "In" Basket.

One reason why catalogs, postcards, sales letters, direct mail packages, brochures, ads, and other printed promotions may be less effective today than they used to is that there are more of them than ever competing for your prospect's attention.

In many markets, your prospects' "in" baskets and mailboxes are filled to overflowing. They have too much to read and not enough time to read it all. Advertising materials have a low priority, behind correspondence, reports, and periodicals.

Using the phone focuses and expedites the selling process. "You get the prospect's undivided attention, if only for three to five minutes, and you usually get a response, even if it's not the one you want," said Bob Woodall, owner of Sales Consultants International, in an interview with *Selling* magazine.

Some prospects find telephone calls intrusive. And in a way, they are. Telephone selling is an "in-your-face" medium. Sure, certain prospects will hang up on you or cut you off. But a percentage will listen. And some of them will buy—usually enough of them to make it worthwhile.

4. The Telephone Is an Interactive, Two-way Marketing Tool.

Aside from the Internet, the telephone is one of the few marketing vehicles that is interactive and allows instantaneous two-way communication between the seller and the prospect. The interactive nature of the telephone enables you to get instant feedback and adjust efforts accordingly.

Scripts and call guidelines can be changed instantly and at virtually no cost to increase response. The ability to ask questions and get immediate answers enables you to qualify prospects on the spot—and more definitively—than almost any other selling method.

When you send out a mailing, you don't know why people respond (or do not respond) the way they do. With telephone selling, your prospects frequently tell you what they think of your product, your offer, you, and the phone call.

As a result, you can immediately respond to objections that, left unanswered, would prevent a sale. You can answer questions, provide additional information, and reason with the person on the other end of the line. In short, you can sell.

This not only increases your chances of selling the current prospect, but also gives you a good feel for how your overall sales approach is working. You can call ten or twenty prospects, analyze the results, and try a different approach on the next ten to twenty people. You can repeat this until you find something that works.

5. Response Is Immediate and Results Can Be Produced Quickly.

You can get orders right on the phone. You can bill customers, ask them to fax a purchase order, or take their credit card information. The result: Fast revenue generation and payback on your telephone selling program.

In addition, telephone salespeople have the opportunity to be more productive than a traditional sales force, because you can phone more prospects in an hour than you can visit in a day. If you have ever been on the road, you know the incredible amount of time wasted in travel and waiting in lobbies. In the time it takes me to drive to my nearest client, I can call ten prospects while sitting at my desk in front of my phone and computer.

6. Telephone Selling Is Relatively Inexpensive.

Making a personal sales call costs one to three hundred dollars or more, depending on how far you have to travel. If the sales call is out of state, you add the cost of travel and lodging.

The cost-per-customer contact for telephone sales ranges from $3 to around $10 or more. This figure factors in the costs of calls that are incomplete, reach voice mail, or otherwise don't get through to the prospect.

Is this reasonable? It compares favorably with face-to-face selling. Direct mail costs 40 to 90 cents for each piece mailed. But that does not include the cost of writing and designing the mailing piece. This can range from a few hundred to many thousands of dollars, depending on the firm you choose and the complexity of the mailing.

Telephone selling costs can be controlled, because you can call 10 people or 200 or 2,000. When you rent a booth at a trade show, on the other hand, you are paying the full price to reach everyone who attends—whether you can sell to them or not. When you take out an ad, you are paying to reach everyone reading that newspaper or magazine—whether they are prospects or not.

Telephone selling is ideal for businesses on a limited budget. You can start a teleselling campaign for less than $500. No major investment in equipment or costly printed promotional materials is required.

Another advantage: If a telephone sales program isn't working, you can find out right away and stop, so time and money aren't wasted. On the other hand, if you mail ten thousand mailers and initial results are poor, it's too late to do anything about it: You've already printed the pieces, rented the list, written the copy, typeset it, taken the photos, and paid a graphic artist to do the layout. Telephone selling can be tested much more inexpensively and rapidly—and the up-front losses in an unsuccessful effort are minimal.

7. It Doesn't Take a Lot of Time.
Yes, many large corporations have a full-time staff dedicated to telephone sales. Others outsource their teleselling to third-party vendors.

But for the average small- to medium-sized business, you can get excellent results without spending a lot of time calling. I can't tell you *exactly* how much time; you'll discover that as you go along. But teleselling doesn't have to be a full-time job.

To estimate how much time you'll have to spend on the phone selling, figure one hour a day, five days a week, for each professional your firm employs. Therefore, in a small accounting firm with three CPAs, each should spend an hour a day making sales calls, and do it every day. If you have a separate person doing the teleselling, that person would need to spend three hours a day on the phone to generate enough work to keep the three accountants busy.

8. It's Not Terribly Complicated.
Basically, teleselling is talking on the phone. It's pretty much the same as selling face to face, except you do it over the phone.

Putting together a direct-mail package, or placing an ad in a magazine, or establishing a Web site on the Internet, can be relatively complex tasks, especially if that's not your full-time job. But we all know how to talk on the telephone, even though some of us may be better at it than others.

There are hardware and software systems you can buy to enhance teleselling. There's even a monthly magazine, *Call Cen-*

ter, to help people keep up with the technology. We'll explore equipment options in chapter 3.

My basic approach is to keep it simple. If you have a phone, you can do teleselling. No special knowledge or technical skills are required. With practice, you can become an adequate or better telephone salesperson.

And you can start right now. It can take weeks to get a large mailing out. Ads for monthly magazines must be placed 6 to 10 weeks in advance. But you can start teleselling tomorrow.

9. Lists Are Readily Available.

Chapter 5 gives details on how to rent, buy, borrow, compile, and use prospecting lists for teleselling. If you know the type of company you want to sell to, and the titles of the prospects you want to reach, chances are there's a list available you can use. If you do not know the titles of the prospects who make decisions about buying the products or services you sell, you will have a more difficult time—but successful teleselling is still quite possible. We'll cover this in detail later.

Be creative in your quest for the ideal list. Use directories. Call mailing list brokers. Obtain membership rosters and lists of seminar and trade-show attendees.

Who are your best prospects? What organizations do they belong to? What conventions do they attend? What publications do they read? What trade shows do they go to? These are the sources for lists that work. A list of some firms that rent telemarketing lists appears on page 75.

10. Teleselling Can Work in Tandem with Other Sales and Marketing Methods for a Synergistic Effect.

Don't feel forced to choose between teleselling and other marketing methods. For many businesses, it makes sense to use the telephone in conjunction with other methods.

Results to direct mailings, for example, can be increased 10 to 25 percent or more when a follow-up call to every prospect is made a week or so after the pieces are mailed. Uses of the telephone in conjunction with other marketing methods include:

- Calling prospects and customers to invite them to a trade show, seminar, or other event
- Calling customers to renew their contract, lease, policy, or subscription as follow-up to a written notice
- Calling people to remind them to attend a sale, party, meeting, seminar, or other event they have already agreed to come to
- Following up with a phone call to everyone who responded to your ad and requested a brochure or catalog of your products
- Following up with prospects after face-to-face sales presentations
- Calling prospects to set up or confirm an appointment
- Taking a survey and following up with information sent via mail
- Calling prospects after purchase to ensure satisfaction with the product or service and to upsell them on additional products
- Letting current customers know about special offers, promotions, discounts, and opportunities
- Updating prospects on new products or new offers
- Periodically reminding customers and prospects about you and your products and services

Here's one other thing to keep in mind: No sales method is perfect. And the telephone is no exception. While using the telephone gives you the advantages we just discussed, there are also some drawbacks you should be aware of.

Disadvantages of Using the Telephone as a Sales Tool

It Can Be Demeaning and Demoralizing If Done Improperly.

Despite the simplicity of teleselling, many people do it the wrong way. By being too aggressive and argumentative, they annoy their prospects and turn them off. The prospects become curt with the tellesellers. There is a lot of rejection and some occasional abuse.

I get many calls from stockbrokers and other financial professionals selling investments. On a recent call, I told the broker politely, "I would be interested in the stocks you describe, but let me stop you because I don't want to waste your time. I do not have the cash to invest right now. I am expecting a few checks from clients and publishers, so why don't you call me in two weeks when I have the money and can act on your ideas?"

I thought this was reasonable, but the telleseller insisted that I let him describe a company he wanted me to buy right then and there. I became irritated. I told him again that I did not have the money to invest, even if I wanted to buy, and besides, I was very busy. To my amazement, he began describing the stock. I hung up.

Another financial services telleseller also could not understand why talking to him about commodities was not the most important thing to me on Earth at the moment he called. When I politely and repeatedly said I did not want more information, he said, irritably, "Mr. Bly, let me ask you a question. Do you object to making a profit?"

I'm sure he felt this line, which he undoubtedly learned in a sales training course on overcoming objections, would dissolve my resistance. My answer to his asinine question was a sarcastic, "That's right, I don't want to make a profit." This stunned him into silence, and when he didn't know what to say next, I ended the call.

Teleselling Creates Opportunities for Rejection.
When you use direct mail or advertising to promote your products or services, there is little rejection involved. Magazine readers don't call the phone number in your ad to tell you they are *not* going to buy. Direct-mail recipients don't send back your order form with a note, "I am not going to order because I don't like your product."

In telephone selling, you hear all the no's as well as the yes's. When prospects don't like you, your product, your service, your company—when they disagree with your sales pitch or are annoyed by the sales call—many will tell you so, in no uncertain terms.

If you sell, you're going to get rejected. Telephone selling is no exception. Don't avoid rejection. If you are not getting rejections, it's probably because you are not making any effort to call new prospects. Rejection is a sign that you are doing the right things, as long as there is a respectable percentage of acceptances along with the rejections.

It's only natural to take rejection personally, to get angry and hurt. Don't. When someone rejects your telephone proposition, he is not rejecting you as a person. He is simply indicating that your product, service, or offer is not right for him at this time. Call another day, and he may buy.

Some tellesellers deserve the rejection they get. The other night, I got a call from a telemarketer selling children's books by mail. The offer: Two free books, and two books on approval. When the saleswoman described the titles, I said I was interested in the offer, but my sons already had one of the books being sent on approval.

No problem, she said. When we get the four books, just send back the one we had already, and pay only for the other books.

This irked me. I didn't want to be sent a book I already owned. I asked if she could send just the one book on approval, or substitute another. To my amazement, she informed me she could not do that. There was no flexibility in the selling process—yet flexibility is a key advantage of teleselling over virtually any other sales or marketing method—and she insisted the company had to ship the book I already owned. Naturally, I passed on their offer.

Rejection gets telesellers feeling down. It is demoralizing to be rejected, to make call after call only to have people hang up or say no every time. Some telesellers act so inappropriately in their desperation to make the sale, they almost demean themselves in the performance of their work.

On the other hand, when you know how to telesell properly, it becomes exciting and gratifying. Yes, people will still hang up, say no, and reject you. But many others will stay on the line, listen, say yes, and buy. When you get a good response to a teleselling effort, calling becomes exciting, because the next call could be your big sale of the month. It's fun!

Many People Dislike Getting Sales Calls.

Just as some people don't like getting direct mail, or watching TV commercials, many people don't like getting telephone sales calls at home or the office. Respect people's preferences and privacy. Accept that some people just don't want to hear from you by phone. If someone doesn't want to talk with you, don't push it. Thank them for their time, and move on to the next call.

Some People Will Be Rude to You.

Some prospects will be abrupt, even rude. This will happen frequently if you are pushy and argumentative; infrequently if you are tactful and respectful. Don't respond to rudeness with more rudeness. Instead, apologize for taking the caller's time, thank her for her patience, and move on to the next call.

If you work for a company as a teleseller, you have especially good reason never to be rude or impolite to a caller. These days, many callers have a caller ID feature on their phone, which gives them your phone number. If you are rude, they may check your number on their caller ID display, call your company back, and complain about you to your boss. Teleselling managers take these complaints very seriously. So don't get into trouble.

Even if you are self-employed, don't be rude to prospects. Remember, many have your number and can call you back or complain about you to the Better Business Bureau or some other authority. You are no longer invisible. Many callers can learn who you are and call *you*. Follow the Golden Rule as stated by Confucius: "What you don't want done to yourself, don't do to others."

Although it may be tempting to do so, never tell prospects they are wrong or imply that they're unwise not to listen to your pitch, take your advice, or buy your product. While you may feel this way, it isn't true, and it will totally turn off the customers.

Why don't more people seem interested? After all, you have a great product or service. But people have other priorities in their lives. Yes, your product might be able to reduce their long-distance phone bill, but did it ever occur to you that reducing their long-distance phone bill may not be the most important thing on their to-do list today or even this week or this month? Think about it from the customer's point of view.

Lack of Prestige.

Although selling has become an important discipline and essential field in the business world—and despite the fact that employers often reward top salespeople far more handsomely than other employees—many people do not have a lot of respect for salespeople. Polls frequently show sales to be one of the least-respected professions. Although you know the value of your skills and your contribution to your company's success, many people will look down on you if they know you are a salesperson, or even if you do telephone selling only part of the time.

Are they correct in their view of you? Of course not. Gone are the days where simply being at the top of your profession, or having the best product, guarantees success. To succeed in today's marketplace, you must sell, market, and promote your products and services—continually and effectively. There is no lack of dignity in this.

The Number of Prospects You Can Reach in an Hour Is Limited.

If you do your own teleselling, the number of prospects you can contact in a day is limited by the number of calls you can make. On the other hand, even a one-person business can reach a virtually unlimited number of prospects through other means—mailings, ads, TV commercials, the Internet—if the business has enough money to fund these promotions.

Teleselling is limited by what telesellers can physically accomplish. Productivity depends on the prospects, the quality of the list, the complexity of the product, the nature of the offer, and the skills of the teleseller. Making eight to twelve calls in an hour is typical of the production rate of many telesellers. Yours may be more or less.

Sometimes Lists Are Not Available.

Although good lists are available for a wide range of markets and industries, in some markets lists are in limited supply or not available at all. If this is the case, you will have difficulty making teleselling pay off for you, and may have to explore an alternate method, such as Yellow Pages advertising.

You May Not Enjoy It.

Some people enjoy teleselling. Some hate it. Most of us vacillate between these two extremes. On days where things are not going well, you may become tired, depressed, and dejected. Picking up the phone to make the next call can become an agonizing effort.

On days where things are going well, you won't want to stop. You'll be thrilled at how you can dial a number, hear someone pick up the phone, and in five or ten minutes, make money by selling them something.

The important thing to remember is this: It doesn't matter how you feel about making your sales calls each day. All that matters is that you do it. If you do it, and follow the procedures in this book, you'll get results. And that should make you happy.

Teleselling Requires Personal Effort and Dedication.

At the beginning, you may be doing most of the calling yourself, especially if you are self-employed or have a small business with limited staff and budget.

When you put an ad in the Yellow Pages, the publisher will design the ad, typeset the copy, and insert it into the book for you. You do nothing. When I send out a mailing, I just hand my secretary the list and it's done, with no effort on my part.

But teleselling is somewhat more labor-intensive than other marketing and sales methods, which is perhaps its greatest drawback. It requires you or another person—an employee or someone you contract to do the work—to sit at a phone with a list of prospects, dial their numbers, make calls, and keep records. If you are not willing to put some effort into it, teleselling is probably not for you.

Once you have some experience, you can train and hire others to make calls on your behalf. But you'll be more effective at hiring and training telesellers if you have performed the task and mastered the skill yourself first. It's hard to teach and motivate people to do something unless you've done it too. And even if your plan is to have others make the calls, you should spend time honing your own skills. You never know when you may need them.

Pick Up the Phone and Dial

You now have an overview of what teleselling is, along with its pros and cons. The rest of this book is written to help you effectively integrate teleselling into your sales and marketing efforts for maximum results. Let's get started.

☎ *Two* ☎

The Elements of Successful Telephone Selling

What does it take to succeed in telephone selling? This chapter presents an overview of the eight basic elements. It also refers you to other chapters for more complete coverage of specific items.

Telephone selling success requires the following:

• *The right environment.* This means having the proper equipment, space, and surroundings for making business phone calls.

• *The right plan.* All telephone selling efforts must follow a plan that includes a target income objective, estimated response rates, and sales call schedule.

• *The right list.* You must get specific, highly targeted calling lists. Using an inadequate list, or not having enough information about the prospects on the list, is a primary cause of teleselling failure.

• *The right words.* Whether you use a script, guidelines, or work without notes, you have to know what to say and how to phrase it. Responses to prospect questions, objections, and comments must be planned out in advance. The rule of thumb is, you should never hear a question to which you don't already know the answer, even if your answer is "I don't know the answer, but I'll get back to you."

• *The right follow-up system.* Actually, if you have any sort of follow-up system, you're a step ahead of most people. The system can include files, software, and other tools that give you a means of keeping track of leads and following up in a diligent manner. It also includes when to follow up, what to say, and how to say it. To succeed in teleselling, you must keep accurate records of your calls and the results.

• *The right skills.* The skills required for teleselling are fairly simple. You have to be able to talk clearly and intelligibly with people on the phone. You must be persuasive without being pushy or obnoxious. You also need the ability to judge situations and people's responses, and act accordingly. Common sense, empathy with people, and a clear speaking voice are valuable assets. Common sense is the asset many tellers either lack or, if they have it, fail to use.

Example: A telemarketer called and began with the ineffective opening, "How are you today?"

"My next-door neighbor's wife died and I am on the way to her funeral," I answered truthfully.

"Great! I'm fine too!" the telemarketer babbled, blindly following the script and ignoring the information I had just given him. Naturally, I hung up on the idiot and bought nothing.

• *The right attitude.* Some people approach selling as a loathsome chore to be avoided at any expense. If this is your attitude, you could be headed for trouble. You don't have to like telephone selling. But you do have to be able to maintain a positive attitude during the time you make your calls each day.

• *Perseverance.* A primary reason for failure is not sticking to the plan. It takes guts, hard work, and strong will to stay on the phone day after day, week after week, even in the face of seeming failure. Those who are persistent eventually succeed; those who give up are certain not to achieve their goals. My experience is that this holds true in most endeavors.

Let's take a look at these eight ingredients of telephone selling success in more detail.

Teleselling Success Element 1:
Setting Up Your Teleselling Center

As with any type of work, the right environment can increase productivity enormously.

Chapter 3 covers hardware, software, and other technical aspects of creating an effective environment for telephone selling. As the use of the telephone increases, selling equipment for telephone call centers has become a big business. Designing and building telephone call centers has become a multimillion-dollar industry. But your telephone calling area need not be elaborate or expensive.

The key is to make the environment fit the people doing the work. If you will be the one making calls, this means setting things up so that *you* are comfortable.

My selling area is my desk. It is in a small rented office on the third floor of a small office building in a quiet New Jersey suburb. I am only one of two offices on the third floor, so there is little noise to disturb me.

Although I will briefly discuss equipment options such as speaker phones and headsets for telesellers, I don't use any of these. I prefer talking on a standard phone.

On my desk I keep a pen and notepad for note taking. I also keep an open file on my computer in case the prospect gives me a lot of details: I can take notes faster typing than by hand.

When you make phone calls and leave messages, people will

call you back. I like to know who is calling before I pick up the phone, so my telephone is equipped with a built-in caller ID feature that displays the caller's telephone number. Chapter 3 discusses the new computer telephone systems that display not only the phone number but also the caller's name, title, and company.

Some telesellers operate out of busy teleselling centers surrounded by other telephone sellers. I prefer more privacy when calling and have designed my office accordingly.

You do not want to be interrupted when speaking with a prospect. If you work in an office, close your door. Put up a DO NOT DISTURB sign. If you are in a cubicle, put up a sign saying you are calling customers and cannot be disturbed. Have a notepad you can use to jot short messages to people who stop by your office while you are on a call, so you do not interrupt the flow of conversation.

Prospects do not appreciate background noise. I have even had clients complain about my air conditioner and the sirens that go off at noon in my town every day. If you work at home, expect people to be intolerant of ringing phones, crying babies, TV and stereo, doorbells, and noisy children. A silent background to phone calls is the professional approach.

When making calls, put the caller first. Tell others to wait. Never put prospects on hold. Especially if *you* called *them*.

Do not have call waiting on your teleselling line. The interruption is extremely annoying to prospects and will turn them off. Instead, get voice mail and call forwarding, so that when you are on the phone with a prospect and another call comes in, it goes to your secretary or voice mail.

The room temperature should be comfortable. I find having the room slightly cold keeps me alert and awake. It can disrupt your flow to ask the prospect to hold so you can take off your sweater or open the window.

Dress as you wish. I prefer comfortable clothes—blue jeans

and sport shirt. Other people tell me they must wear business clothes to feel professional. It's up to you.

A speaker at a sales seminar said that every telephone salesperson should place a mirror on the wall. You can see yourself as you talk, and you should always be smiling. The rationale: Smiling lifts your mood and makes you come across more enthusiastically.

While I have found this to be true, I don't bother with the mirror. However, if I feel I am in a negative mood or am getting frustrated with the prospect, I force a smile, and it does work!

TELESELLING SUCCESS ELEMENT 2: PLANNING—THE PROFESSIONAL APPROACH

After 16 years in business, I have mixed feelings about planning. The conventional wisdom is that you need a written plan to keep yourself on track and reach your goal. Many studies have shown that people who have written goals and objectives are more successful than those of us who do not.

On the other hand, some of the planning advocates overdo it. Small businesses can't spend half a year writing a plan; they have too much work to do. And it's a fact that many successful entrepreneurs built their businesses without a heavy reliance on formal planning; it's simply not their style.

Too many corporate managers and executives are obsessed with planning—so much so that they spend all of their time writing plans, memos, and reports, and consequently do not make any real business progress. Do not allow planning to become a theoretical exercise. Too many planners view the outcome of planning as the plan. That's wrong. The outcome of planning should be business success. The plan is just the means to the end. Nothing more.

For telephone selling, however, you do need a plan. Why?

Without a plan, there is simply no way to know how many phone calls you must make each day to generate the revenue your business requires.

Fortunately, doing this type of plan is simple. It requires just a little thought and can be completed in under an hour. There is no long-winded theoretical document involved. You just need to know where you are going and what you have to do to get there.

Chapter 4 gives complete instructions on how to create a workable, practical telephone selling plan. The elements are simple. In essence, you must determine how much revenue you want to generate, figure out how many calls per day are required to meet that objective, and then make those calls. It really is that simple.

TELESELLING SUCCESS ELEMENT 3: THE IMPORTANCE OF THE LIST

While I may come across as being almost too much of an advocate for telephone selling, the fact is I do use and practice other sales and marketing methods. In fact, my background is in direct mail, not face-to-face selling. I got involved in teleselling when I used the telephone to follow up on leads generated by direct mail, and to upgrade orders taken over inbound 800 telephone lines. Then I discovered that in some instances you could get good results by calling people directly, without doing a mailing first.

People often ask what element of the mailing—the copy, the design, the paper stock, the colors, the format—is the most important. The answer: The mailing list. Response rates generated by different direct-mail packages for the same product can vary by 10, 20, even 50 percent or more. But when we mail the same package to different lists, we find that the response rate of the best-pulling list can exceed the response rate of the worst-pulling list by a factor of ten or more!

Similarly, telephone selling requires a good list. Chapter 5 tells what to look for in telephone selling lists, where to find them, and how to buy or rent them.

You want complete information on the prospects—name, job title, company, phone number, address, and any other available details, such as whether they buy your type of product, their budget, their needs, and so on.

You want accurate information. This means having a list that is updated on a regular basis. Since people today move and change jobs frequently, old lists tend to contain many outdated names and phone numbers—and calling people incorrectly listed wastes your time.

You want a list of the right prospects. If you sell ad specialties, for example, you could use a list of local businesses compiled from the Yellow Pages. But you would get better results with a list of prospects who were known to buy and use premiums and incentives on a regular basis. Using the techniques I will reveal in chapter 5, you would discover that such a list actually exists, and you could obtain it to dramatically enhance sales response.

If you already use lists for direct mail, be aware that more and more of these lists are now available on telemarketing cards or as computer printouts with telephone numbers. Most mailing list brokers also handle telemarketing lists. Check the Yellow Pages under "Mailing Lists," "Direct Mail," or "Mailing List Brokers."

Some list brokers offer free catalogs describing the lists available for rental. One such broker is Edith Roman Associates in New York City. For a free catalog, call 800-223-2194. I use their lists frequently and recommend them highly.

Do not assume that just because two lists seem similar, they will yield similar results. Once I did a sales campaign to computer professionals who use VAX (Digital Equipment) systems. There are two similar magazines in the field, and we tested subscriber lists of both magazines. One pulled three times the response of the other, although to me the magazines seemed almost identical.

TELESELLING SUCCESS ELEMENT 4: SCRIPTS AND CALL GUIDELINES

What type of script or notes should you use? It's up to you. Some people read from a script that is either printed on paper or appears on a computer screen in front of them. Usually people who read scripts are thought of as telemarketers, not tellesellers. That is, they recite a rote sales pitch from which they cannot and do not deviate.

The main advantage of the telemarketing approach is that it allows you to test scripts, offers, and sales arguments scientifically. Because there is no deviation, and every telephone representative says virtually the same thing, you can quickly test different script approaches to see which is best. Also, because telemarketing requires less training, minimal product knowledge, and fewer sales skills, your training costs, salaries, and commissions are reasonably low.

The main disadvantage of the telemarketing approach is that people reading from a script often sound like robots. There is a phoniness and lack of sincerity that comes across when reading a script, unless you are very, very good at it. People can usually detect when the telephone salesperson is reading from a script, and many find it a turnoff.

Another disadvantage of telemarketing is that the telephone representatives lack extensive product knowledge or sales skills. Therefore they are limited in the way they can handle a prospect who is not buying into the pitch.

With telephone selling, the person doing the selling must be fairly knowledgeable about the product, market, and customers.

The teleseller must be able to respond to situations, answer questions, address objections, and provide detailed information on the product or service being offered. With these capabilities, tellers are better able to deal with prospects on an individual level than telemarketers.

Teleselling is more of an individual, one-on-one selling situation, similar in many respects to face-to-face selling. Tellers can react flexibly to respond to whatever the prospect says.

Telemarketing, despite the fact that it involves talking on the phone to prospects one at a time, is more of a mass medium, similar to direct mail, in that the copy is scripted and inflexible.

Most telemarketers use scripts. Most tellers use call guidelines or notes that remind them of key points and enable them to instantly reference the right phrase or response to any question, comment, or objection.

Some tellers prefer to work without notes of any kind. This becomes possible with practice and repetition. After you make a certain number of calls, you've heard all the questions and objections, and you have the answers at the top of your head. After a while you know what to say, and the right words roll off your tongue.

As a rule, the less scripted the call, and the fewer notes you rely on, the more natural you will sound. And this is what you want. People like to buy from other people, not from robots.

When you get started, use as many notes or as comprehensive a script as you feel comfortable with. But you will reach a point when you feel the script or notes are superfluous. When you get that feeling, put the script or notes aside (not out of reach; just aside) and try making some calls without these support materials. You'll find the quality of your conversation jumps to a whole new level of effectiveness.

Even those of us who work without notes or scripts have at one time written out or scripted all or part of our sales presentation. You should too. The exercise helps you determine what you will say in each situation and the best way to say it. You shouldn't stumble over any part of your script. If you do, rewrite it to make it more conversational.

Chapters 6 through 8 cover scripting and call guidelines for a wide range of selling situations. Read the sample bits of dialogue aloud. If you can think of a better or more natural way to get the message across, write it down.

The idea is to capture the essence of the message. If you want to use the scripts word for word and that works for you, fine. But if saying things in your own words feels more comfortable to you, I urge you to do so.

Teleselling Success Ingredient 5: Following Up for Maximum Results

Follow-up is so essential to sales success that I have devoted chapter 10 to a complete discussion of the topic.

Two key points. First, you need a follow-up system that is automatic. That is, when you come into the office, you simply check a file, launch a PC program, glance at a calendar, or look in a book and you automatically get a list of whom you must call that day, why, and what you are supposed to say to them.

More sales fall through the cracks because of poor or missed follow-up than almost any other reason.

Keep your promises to your prospects. If you say you will send material, do so promptly. If you say you will call back on a specific date, call on that day. If you don't, your prospect may buy from your competitor instead of you—simply because he was there and you weren't.

Calling once—sending your brochure one time and then waiting for the prospects to come to you—isn't sufficient to generate the sales you need. Think about all the brochures you've been mailed, all the business cards you've been handed. How many are lost, misfiled, or thrown away? How many of these people can you recall from your memory?

The more time that has passed since the prospect spoke with you, the more you fade from her awareness. Periodic follow-up is necessary to remind her that you exist, and to make sure she thinks of you first when a need for your product or service does arise.

Follow-up should serve as a useful reminder to the prospect. Ideally, it should be viewed as a customer service, not a sales effort. For instance, when the dentist sends you a postcard saying it's time for your checkup and cleaning, you appreciate it. A customer service? Yes. But primarily, dentists send such cards to generate more business.

On the other hand, we've all experienced the teleseller who calls too often and follows up too frequently. Your follow-ups should be frequent enough that the prospect maintains awareness of you, but not so frequent that you are perceived as a pest.

Too many follow-up calls when not needed make prospects uncomfortable with you. They begin to resent the calls and reach a point where they deliberately make a decision not to buy from you, precisely because you pester them.

Chapter 10 covers how to find the right frequency for follow-up. Follow-up schedules should be tailored to each individual prospect. Although the chapter discusses various schools of thought and rules of thumb concerning follow-up frequency, use these as guidelines only.

The best strategy is to let the prospect indicate what frequency of contact is appropriate. Directly or indirectly, people will let you know if you are calling too often.

If you are, schedule fewer calls. Consider making some of your follow-up contacts through alternative means such as e-mail, fax, letter, or postcard. Instead of picking up the phone, drop a note or article reprint of interest in the mail. Use the telephone, but don't overdo it, or you risk offending the prospect.

Teleselling Success Element 6: Building Your Phone and Sales Skills

The primary skill you need is the ability to say the right words at the right time, in a manner that is natural, friendly, nonadversarial, and not off-putting to prospects.

As discussed, you will develop a script or call guidelines or notes giving you the right words.

You will gain the ability to recall and say these words at the right time through repetition, or by mastering your use of notes or scripts.

You will gain the ability to say these things in a natural, non-salesman-like way through experience.

The more calls you make, the better you will get. There are certain disciplines that are only mastered by doing. Making telephone sales calls is one of them. (Public speaking is another.) At first, you will feel awkward, although surprisingly, your prospects won't realize how nervous, uncomfortable, or inexperienced you are. You always sound worse to yourself than you do to other people.

Within a few days, you'll start to become comfortable with calling up strangers on the phone and talking with them. Within a few weeks, you'll relax and loosen up, and your results will perceptibly improve. Even when you're first starting, you're not as bad as you think you are. And you will only get better with practice.

The best telephone selling technique is to have no technique. Don't try to imitate sales trainers you hear on audio sales training tapes. Don't intentionally pace your speech, or change your volume for effect, as speaking and acting coaches might tell you to do. It's phony, and when you speak in a phony manner, it comes across to the person on the other end of the line.

The best strategy is to be yourself. Be sincere. Be genuine. Be a person. Let your natural personality and style shine through in

31

your conversations. People like dealing with people. The more you come across as a real person, the better your chances of making a connection with the prospect. People do business with people they like.

Talking on the phone comes easily and naturally to some people. Others find it an uncomfortable and difficult chore. But I believe almost anyone can learn to become a reasonably competent teleseller in a reasonably short period of time.

Some people are naturally "good" with people on the phone. My mother is one of them. These lucky people do not need a lot of training or practice to be successful in telephone sales. However, the more calls they make, the better they'll get.

Others may require more polish. Training seminars can be helpful. But the only way to master this skill and make it your own is to do it. For the majority of activities we engage in at the office and at home, everything from making speeches to ice skating, instruction can help guide you, but practice—doing the thing repeatedly and regularly for a prolonged period—is what sets the pros apart from the amateurs. Telephone selling included.

TELESELLING SUCCESS ELEMENT 7: ATTITUDE

You must have a positive attitude. That doesn't mean you have to enjoy teleselling. It doesn't mean you have to feel good about making the phone calls. It simply means you must be enthusiastic, energetic, and optimistic while making the calls. How you feel before or after that is up to you and doesn't affect the quality of your teleselling efforts.

But having a good attitude while *on* the phone is essential. The reason: How you feel is reflected in your voice, and prospects pick up on it. If you're angry or depressed or bored, you will come across as hostile, negative, or uncaring. If you're enthusiastic, your enthusiasm will show through in your conversation, and prospects will be more inclined to listen.

Always be your most pleasant self. If you do this, and nothing else, you will be far ahead of the pack. Rudeness is rampant in today's society. Telesellers and telemarketers often don't enjoy their work, and this frequently shows through in their attitude, tone, even the words they use. Be sincere, enthusiastic, polite, friendly, tolerant, patient, understanding, and kind.

Remember, you are interrupting people at work or leisure. Put yourself in their position. Yes, your product or service may be able to help them. In fact, it may be the perfect solution to their problems. But they aren't idiots just because they don't instantly agree with you or see the value of what you're discussing.

When you call them, they're thinking of something else, and the first thing you must do is focus their attention away from what is immediately in front of them, if you can, to the proposition you want to discuss. Because you are imposing on their time, this must be done politely and gently.

Your prospects do not owe you a living. How much money you make this month is of no concern to them. Their only interest is in buying goods and services that deliver the benefits they want at a price they can afford.

They are not aware how important it is to you to make the sale, nor would they act any differently if they were aware of it. Your problems are simply not of concern to them. Their problems, needs, and requirements are paramount.

The positive attitude should permeate the entire call, from initial dialing through the end of the conversation. Avoid the mistake many telesellers make of abruptly hanging up on prospects who say they are not interested; it gives a bad impression of you in particular and the telephone selling industry as a whole.

I suppose telesellers hang up on me either because they don't want to waste time once they discover I'm not buying today, or else they do it in annoyance. But I didn't call them. They called me—uninvited. Even if I'm not interested or don't have time to listen to their message, I still expect to be treated in a courteous, professional manner. So do your prospects.

Making telephone calls to prospects can be frustrating. It's only natural to get steamed. But you are doing the selling. The other people are doing the buying. They will decide whether you get the order. They can be difficult if they want, and still buy. If you are difficult, you will not get an order.

Here is a fact that will help you find a comfortable attitude: People do things for their reasons, not yours. The fact that you want to make a sale, or you genuinely feel they would benefit from the product, is immaterial. What's important to your prospects are their needs, their wants, their hopes, their problems, their fears, their dreams.

People's buying is triggered by two basic motivations: to gain reward or benefits, or to avoid loss, pain, or punishment. For example, you buy a schedule planner to gain the reward of saving time. You buy insurance to avoid financial loss. You buy aluminum siding to avoid having to paint your house every few years.

If your prospects don't greatly desire the particular benefits your product delivers—or if they do not feel the pain of the problem they have and it can solve sharply enough—they will not buy. All you can do is identify the desire or pain, amplify it, and then offer your product as the solution. You cannot create desire or pain where it does not exist.

Timing is essential. Making a particular sale is largely a matter of timing. Sometimes you call prospects at a moment when they happen to need exactly what you are selling. At those times, the sale happens much more easily.

Most times, the prospects are not focused on the issues you are addressing in your call. If they are too busy or distracted, it is difficult to get them to stop thinking about their immediate concern and concentrate on your proposal.

If you sell expensive equipment, and the prospects just spent their entire budget buying a similar system from your competitor, it is unlikely that they will throw their investment away and buy the same or similar equipment from your company. You have to reach the prospects at the right time in their buying cycle.

Since you don't know the prospects' buying cycle, it's difficult to reach them at the right time. A certain percentage of calls will reach them at the ideal time; a larger percentage won't.

The trick is to ask about their buying cycle on the initial call, so your follow-up efforts have a better chance of reaching them at the appropriate time. If prospects say they are not interested, find out when would be a good time to call back. If they are not buying supplies now, find out how much inventory they have and when they expect to run out. Then call them in advance of this date so you have a shot at getting the order before they reorder from their current supplier.

Here's a technique that works in the closing stage of the sales cycle when the prospect is evaluating your product along with the products of your competitors. If a prospect indicates she is still thinking about it and hasn't made up her mind, and you get no indication that you are likely to be the winner (or the prospect indicates you are unlikely to be chosen), say the following:

"Ms. Prospect, could you do me a favor? Whatever your decision—our product or someone else's—let's talk *one more time* before you sign the contract." Ask when the prospect will be making a decision. Then set an appointment to call back a few days before then. And do so.

The benefit is that you are given one last chance to make a sale you would not otherwise have been given. Something could go wrong that turns the prospect off the other supplier. If you don't call, she'll let it pass and buy anyway from the first supplier. If you do, she may give you a more serious second look.

It's important to call before the deal is closed. Once the

paperwork is signed, a prospect will almost never cancel the contract to go with another vendor. Your best bet then is finding out when the company will evaluate the product or service, and make a decision about continuing. Find out the date, set a return call prior to that, and make the call.

TELESELLING SUCCESS ELEMENT 8: PERSISTENCE

As a teleseller, you will make many calls that do not produce the response you would have wished for. People will be too busy to talk, too uninterested, too preoccupied. Your product will not be right for them. Or it will be right for them, but they do not wish to make a purchase decision right now.

The tendency is to give up. Don't. The Number One reason for failure in selling is failure to stick to the sales plan. It takes guts, hard work, and a strong will to stay on the phone day after day, week after week, even in the face of seeming failure.

"Too often, ambitious people with dreams and talent fall short—even flat on their faces—because they give up too soon," writes the motivational speaker Roscoe Barnes III in his book *Discover Your Talent and Find Fulfillment* (Gettysburg, Pa.: McKinley & Henson, 1992). "One of the keys to success is determination. A person needs determination to succeed in anything. Sometimes you have to grit your teeth, clench your fists, and refuse to give up."

Those who are persistent in sales eventually succeed. Those who give up fail to achieve their objective.

"Press on," said Calvin Coolidge. "Nothing in the world can take the place of persistence. Talent will not; nothing is more common than unsuccessful men with talent. Genius will not; unrewarded genius is almost a proverb. Education will not; the world is full of educated derelicts. Persistence and determination alone are omnipotent."

The sales trainer Paul Karasik says that sales is like a fifteen-round boxing match in which 90 percent of salespeople give up during Round 14. "If they would only stay on their feet and keep slugging for one more round, they'd be standing at the final bell," notes Karasik. Winston Churchill put it this way: "Never give up."

Do not let rejection stop you. "Be it sport or business, you don't excel until you've been knocked around a little," says Chip Ganassi, a race-car driver and winning owner. When you get rejected, you learn how to do the calls better so the next person says yes.

Certainly you want good results. If you are not getting them, don't give up. Instead, try something different. Or intensify your efforts. Or do both.

Sometimes salespeople have dry spells where nothing seems to work out. Other times, they can't write up the orders fast enough to keep up with demand.

I find it is usually rain or shine, feast or famine, in sales. The dry spells and the busy periods usually balance themselves out. So don't give up if you start with a dry spell, even a long one. It will break, and success will come.

Persistence pays. Many of your competitors fail because they give up too early. The more effort you make, the greater the results.

Many salespeople are like the job hunters who complain, "I responded to three help-wanted ads and didn't get any interviews." If you want to get interviews, send out 300 letters, not three. Likewise, if you want to generate business on the phone, make 300 calls, not 3 or 30.

There are only two ways to increase your teleselling productivity. One is to improve these ratios. Try a different approach to increase your percentage response when generating leads or converting inquiries to sales. Every percentage-point increase means more sales and less work for you.

The second way to increase sales is to step up your selling efforts. Instead of making 10 calls a day, make 11 or 12. That's just one or two extra calls per day. You can do that, can't you? Even if your ratios stay the same, this will increase your sales volume 10 to 20 percent. A famous person (I forget who) once said, "The more work I do, the more successful I get." Persistence and effort are not the only ingredients for teleselling success, but they are key ingredients.

Many people approach their sales tasks with fear and discomfort. What about you? If you have a lot riding on the success of your telephone selling efforts, then it's only natural to be nervous.

Am I telling you not to be afraid? No. As motivational speaker and sales trainer Dr. Rob Gilbert says, "Courage is not the absence of fear. Courage is feeling the fear and doing it anyway." It doesn't matter how you feel about telephone selling. All that matters is what you *do*.

As a rule, it's better to do something than nothing. Too many people do nothing. Or they do something, but not enough. Discussing her success in sales, Jane Trahey, a Chicago advertising executive, once told me, "I like to have a lot of balls up in the air at one time. This increases the odds that at least one will stick."

A tremendous mistake is to have too low a level of sales and marketing activity. If your response rate is one positive response for every 20 calls, and you make just five calls today, your chances of hearing "yes" today will be only one in four. However, if you make 40 calls, you are likely to produce two new leads or acquire two new customers. The greater your effort, the better your results.

We talked about the importance of sticking with your calling plan. This is important when things are slow. But it is equally important to maintain your call activity when business is good.

The tendency of most small businesses is to stop selling and marketing when sales are good and the company is busy. That's only natural. But it's a mistake.

The reason? For most of us, the sales cycle ranges from several weeks to several months or more. Therefore, by continuing to market and sell today, when we are busy, we generate leads and prospects who will become customers later on, just as we are finishing up our current work.

Continual sales and marketing is the best way to ensure a steady flow of orders at a relatively high level. If you stop marketing while you're busy, there's a good chance you'll have no orders coming in once the current peak period is over. You'll get peaks and valleys in sales volume, rather than the steady, continuous high you want.

Even if you already have all the business you need for now and the foreseeable future, it's still a good idea to continue with your sales plan. Why? When you have more prospects than you can handle, you can pick and choose. You can do business with those who fit best in terms of need, personality, and budget, and enjoy the luxury of turning the rest away.

And by generating more demand for your product or service than there is supply, you eliminate the need to negotiate and lower prices, as so many of your competitors do. When people are lined up to buy, checkbook in hand, you can set your price and stick with it. This increases not only your gross sales but also your profit margins.

Three

Creating an Effective Telephone Selling Center

In my nearly two decades in business I have become convinced that having a comfortable, well-organized work space suitable to your personality and work style can result in a major improvement in your personal productivity. If you're doing telephone sales, this means that having the right work environment can help you make more calls and therefore increase your sales.

Telephone and teleselling equipment is a big industry today. Many articles are written about why you must use a certain headset, computer program, or terminal.

Do not feel you have to do what others are doing. Do what works best for you. An example: Many telephone salespeople are fond of using telephone headsets, available in any telephone store. Headsets, which can be worn like the headphones of a stereo, enable you to make calls with your hands free.

Some telephone salespeople use headsets because they find it more comfortable than resting the telephone handset in the crook of their neck, as I often do. Certainly it does keep your hands free. And if you are on the phone frequently, it can prevent neck cramps.

But I don't use a telephone headset, and you may not want to either. When I'm wearing one, I'm acutely aware that I'm a telephone salesperson calling people to sell them something—and that's not how I want to feel.

As I've said earlier, you have the greatest success talking to prospects on the phone when you act like a regular person, not a salesperson or a telemarketer. Since I make my regular business and personal calls using an ordinary phone set, I use an ordinary phone to make my sales calls as well. It feels more natural, like making a call to your best friend, favorite customer, or your spouse. When I'm wearing a headset, I can't help feeling like Betty, the Time-Life operator—somewhat robotic and impersonal. So I don't use them.

I'm also at a loss to understand how telemarketers do their jobs effectively in the typical telemarketing "boiler room," with half a dozen or more telemarketers sitting next to each other in tiny cramped cubicles, simultaneously calling from a list of prospects. I would also feel nervous with a telemarketing supervisor walking around the room watching me as I work.

My best work is done in peace and quiet. Solitude is essential. In my first job, I shared a single office with five other people, and I hated it. When I was offered a job by another company, I put it in my contract that I would be given my own office with a door I could close.

Several large corporations have measured employee response to an improvement in the quality and comfort of surroundings. One study showed that changing an uncomfortable, unattractive space into a comfortable, attractive office reduced absenteeism in large companies 15 percent.

Why You Need a Well-Designed Area for Telephone Selling

There are two important reasons why your work space must suit you.

First, tellesellers must be free of interruptions. You must give your prospect your full attention. Even though you are busy and pressured, the impression must be that the most important thing in your day is talking with them.

Occasionally when I am talking with a prospect or customer on the phone, a messenger or other delivery person will knock on my door. This simple act throws me off and is interruptive, and the prospects can get annoyed. Worse, even though the messengers see that I am on the phone, many of them stand around looking at me, waiting for me to either put the call on hold to talk to them or for me to finish. This is distracting and annoying.

The best strategy: A DO NOT DISTURB sign on your cubicle or office door. If you work in a small office, instruct Federal Express, Airborne, and UPS to leave the package if you are busy. Some delivery services allow you to sign a blanket release so that packages can be left without signature. For others, you can keep a signed air bill posted to your door.

If it's a choice between being abrupt with the person standing there or with the person on the phone, be abrupt with the person standing there—unless he or she is also a customer or prospect. Never make a prospect feel as if you are rushing a call or doing the call simultaneously with other activities.

The second reason it's important to have a good work space is productivity. Although you are sitting down when making phone calls, it's tiring. You have to be alert, continually listen, formulate quick responses, take notes, and sometimes retrieve information on the fly. Pulling product literature, recording information, or filling out papers can fatigue you and slow you down. When everything is in it's right place, easy to find and use, you expend less effort on the paperwork aspects of telephone selling, and so remain fresher and more alert during the calling.

EQUIPMENT

Telephone selling does not require a lot of equipment. True, you could easily spend five thousand dollars or more on a computer, special phone, and software. But it's not necessary. All you really need is a phone, a chair, and a desk.

Add additional equipment as budget allows and only if you feel it will really help you. Keep in mind that a lot of office equipment can be leased, then purchased once the lease runs out if you want to keep it. Most software can be used on approval for 30 days. Many telephone companies offer a risk-free 30-day trial period for relatively inexpensive items such as phones and caller ID boxes. If you want to lease a computer system and need a source for financing, call Studebaker-Worthington Leasing Corporation toll-free at 800-645-7232. If you are ordering equipment from out of town and need special shipping or handling, call Associated High-Tech at 800-645-8300.

When you get something new, use it right away, before the trial period expires. If you don't like it, send it back.

Okay. Let's talk about the basic equipment.

Telephone and Phone Features

You already have a phone. And it's probably good enough for your needs. If not, get a quality phone set from any reliable manufacturer. AT&T phones are excellent. So are Northern Telecom and Cidco.

If you are getting a new phone or upgrading your phone system, consider getting equipment offering the following features:

• *Push-button dialing.* Rotary phones are obsolete. If you have one, get rid of it. You are wasting too much time dialing. And rotary phones can't navigate through the menus of many of your prospects' voice-mail systems.

• *An LED display.* This displays the status of various features and functions.

• *Caller ID.* When you have caller ID, the display can identify the source of incoming calls. Some regional telephone companies offer caller ID that shows you the name of the caller or his company as well as the phone number. You can decide whether to take the call, or have call forwarding or voice mail handle it.

Caller ID presentation is especially valuable to tellers who screen calls. It is also useful for help desks, support lines, customer-service departments, and other departments who can respond more professionally when they know in advance who is calling. Caller ID works with call forwarding, call waiting, and three-way calling.

• *Memory dial.* You can store important phone numbers in memory and dial them at the push of a button. This can significantly cut down dialing time when you call your most important prospects and customers.

• *ISDN compatibility.* ISDN, short for integrated services digital network, is an internationally accepted standard for high-speed data communication. ISDN lines transmit data at higher rates than regular telephone lines and thus can save you time and reduce phone bills when you communicate with customers by modem, e-mail, on-line services, fax, and the Internet.

• *Multiple lines.* Your customers should never get a busy signal when they call you. One solution is to use voice mail. For a small monthly fee, you can get voice-mail service. When you are on the phone, calls can be forwarded to a voice mailbox which takes the caller's message. An alternative is to have more than one phone line. You can get a phone that can handle two different phone lines (with two different numbers) for under $150. You'll probably want separate lines anyway for your phone, fax, and modem.

• *Conference calling.* Some prospects may want to include other people on the call. If they have a speaker phone, they can gather around it in a conference room. If they don't, you can use the conference calling feature (called three-way calling by some telephone companies) to call multiple parties and link them in a conference call. One such service is SHAREcall, available from AT&T.

• *Redial.* When you get a busy signal or have another problem when dialing, just hit the redial button. The phone will automatically redial the number for you, saving you time and effort.

• *"Hold" button.* Avoid using your hold button. You should not put prospects on hold once you have called them. A better alternative is to have incoming calls routed to another phone or to a voice mailbox.

• *Extra function keys.* Get a phone with some extra function keys, so there are some keys that do nothing. This allows you to add new services and features as they become available without upgrading or replacing your existing telephone equipment.

• *Extra-length cord.* If you like to get up, stretch your legs, and walk around while you talk on the phone, get an extra-long phone cord, at least six feet. A short cord, if bent and twisted, may also cause a crackling or interruption on the phone line.

• *Headset.* As I've said, I don't like them, but many swear by them. The advantage is that it leaves your hands completely free to make notes, pull files, and use your computer while you talk.

• *Speaker phones.* Use the speaker phone only when you need to have a group of people sitting around a table participate in a call. Don't use your speaker phone for regular one-on-one calls; the voice quality is inferior to that of a regular phone handset.

• *Voice-activated dialing.* Speech recognition enables callers to dial numbers by saying the number, dial specific parties by speaking the person's name, and automatically identify themselves to the network by voice, without having to remember or punch in a personal identification number. It saves you time when dialing and eliminates the need to carry an ID card or telephone directory.

• *Message waiting indicator.* Users are automatically alerted when they have messages waiting for them in voice mail. Notification can take place via a message on the phone's LED display or an audible tone. The need for users to call in to see whether they have voice-mail messages is eliminated.

• *Single-number reach.* If you have multiple phones—several business phones, a cellular phone, home phone—single-number reach enables callers to reach you by calling a single number. This eliminates the need for them to remember multiple numbers when they want to track you down.

• *Call transfer.* Allows you to transfer calls to other people within your office, ideal if you work with other tellers. Use it to transfer calls meant for others in your company, eliminating the need to ask the caller to call back.

• *Do not disturb.* You can set your phone to automatically route calls to another phone (such as your assistant's or secretary's) or to your voice mailbox if you want to work undisturbed.

• *Selective call acceptance.* A variation of "do not disturb," this feature allows certain calls to get through your "do not disturb" screen, on the basis of the caller's phone number or ID, meaning that you can avoid calls you do not want to get while being sure that important prospects can reach you at all times.

• *Voice message retrieval.* Lets you retrieve your voice-mail messages from phones other than your own. Useful for tellers who sometimes attend meetings outside the office.

• *Call forwarding.* Call forwarding means the phone forwards (sends) the call to another phone. You can have calls forwarded immediately, when the caller receives a busy signal, or when the phone rings but is not answered.

• *Call waiting.* Allows a single phone on one phone line simultaneously to receive multiple calls. If you are on the phone, and another party dials your number, you hear a beep tone, which lets you know that someone else is calling. By pressing a key, you can put the first call on hold and take the second call or can toggle back and forth between the two calls at will. You can also ignore the call or combine call waiting with another service to have the second call picked up and answered by voice mail. This feature is not, however, one you should have on your teleselling line, as I've already said.

Which features are available in your area code depends on what your phone company is currently offering. Call them for details.

Do You Need a Cellular Phone?

If you have other responsibilities aside from teleselling, these duties may take you away from the office. Yet you still want to be accessible to your prospects when they call. A cellular phone may be the answer.

Cell phones, once a status symbol for wealthy individuals and high-powered corporate executives, are increasingly more common today. According to the Cellular Telecommunications Industry Association (CTIA), there will be as many as 86 million wireless-phone users by the year 2000.

Here are some features to look for when selecting a cellular phone and a wireless service provider:

• *Sleep mode.* Subscribers can now leave their mobile units on without wasting battery power. In sleep mode, the mobile phone automatically turns off its receiver while idle and periodically checks for messages.

With sleep mode, batteries in mobile phones can last longer, eliminating the need for frequent recharging. Subscribers miss fewer calls, increasing air-time revenue. Heavy talkers—subscribers who rely heavily on wireless services for incoming calls and messages—conserve precious battery power while leaving mobiles on all the time.

• *Short-message service (SMS).* This feature permits cellphone and land-line users to send alphanumeric messages of approximately 80 characters to wireless subscribers; the messages are displayed on the LED of the recipient's mobile phone. These messages allow the mobile-phone-end user to receive important information even when the mobile phone is in use without answering or making a call to voice mail.

SMS can replace conventional pagers for many messaging applications. If executives in important meetings can't be interrupted, and you both have SMS, you can send them an urgent—and complete—message on their alphanumeric display. A salesperson on the road can receive key figures without having to take a call or jot them down.

• *Authentication.* This feature interferes with thieves' attempts to duplicate and use other people's mobile identification numbers. The subscriber's mobile-phone ID is scrambled and mixed with lengthy random numbers. This makes it difficult for thieves to get onto the network, which in turn can reduce revenues lost from phone fraud. Extensive network interworking is supported.

• *Enhanced registration.* When a call is made to a mobile subscriber, the network finds the mobile phone and forwards the call. With enhanced registration, the network can more easily locate mobile phones and forward calls more quickly. If the mobile phone is turned off, the mobile switching center initiates secondary call treatment, such as call forwarding, voice mail, or messaging. With enhanced registration, subscribers register every time their mobile unit is turned on or off or when they leave a predetermined area, such as their home serving territory. The network knows where mobile subscribers are, so calls can be connected rapidly. This increases call-completion rates.

Enhanced registration provides value-added service to subscribers who can't afford to be out of touch with their offices, colleagues, and customers. These include salespeople, field technicians, doctors, contractors, service people, insurance agents, and other mobile professionals.

There are many wireless service providers to choose from. I highly recommend AT&T Wireless Services.

Answering Machine, Voice-Mail, Telephone-Answering Services

You can get a good answering machine for $50 to $125 at any electronics store such as Radio Shack. Check *Consumer Reports* to see which machines are rated most reliable, since you don't want to risk missing calls.

The machine should allow you to check for messages remotely either with a beeper device you carry or by dialing in from a touch-tone phone and entering an ID code. You also want flexibility in the length of both the announcement message and the recorded messages.

If your phone company offers inexpensive voice-mail service available from its central office, my feeling is this is a better alternative, and you can use it instead of having an answering machine. When the tape jams or the power goes off, your answering machine won't answer, but voice mail always will. Also, it eliminates the expense of buying a new answering machine to replace your old, worn one every few years. Also eliminated is the hassle of cleaning the machine, replacing worn tapes, and other servicing.

Another alternative is telephone answering services. These

were more popular in the days when it was considered "unprofessional" to let a machine answer a business phone line. With the tremendous growth in voice-mail usage, having machines answer phones has become a commonplace and well-accepted practice. Therefore you should use a telephone answering service only because you prefer it. Answering machines and voice-mail systems are now considered appropriate and acceptable.

When you have incoming calls, consider picking up the phone yourself. It mildly surprises and often impresses prospects. With caller ID, you can always choose not to pick up the phone if you get a call from someone with whom you don't want to speak right now.

If you are at a larger company, and the phone is answered by a receptionist or department secretary, it is only natural to want to screen calls. Resist having telephone personnel screen calls too rigorously, and make sure they do the screening in a polite, friendly, nonadversarial way.

Too often receptionists and other telephone personnel today treat every caller as a suspected telemarketer. This may backfire when the person calling you and subjected to this grilling is, in fact, a potential customer. It is a big turnoff and can rapidly turn a warm call cold.

WORK SPACE

We have already discussed the importance of a comfortable and adequately equipped work space.

Make sure the lighting, temperature, and any background noise in your work area is to your liking at all times. You do not want to have to interrupt a telephone sales call to get up and open the window or turn down the air-conditioning. At the same time, you want to be comfortable while talking; otherwise, you'll find yourself rushing your prospects off the phone so you can get a drink of water or go to the bathroom.

Since you'll be sitting all day, get a comfortable chair. Bob Moshman offers this tip in his manual, *Home Incorporated:* When shopping for chairs, put your hand on the chair seat and press down firmly. If you can feel the structure of the chair through the seat, the cushion is not well padded enough and will not provide comfortable sitting for long periods.

Prospect files should be within arm's reach so you can readily pull them if a client or prospect calls. Having the right information in front of you when speaking to a prospect creates an aura of professionalism and gives prospects confidence in you.

You can keep files in a Pendaflex file holder within reach of your desk chair. Or you can computerize your prospect files.

CHOOSING A COMPANY NAME THAT WILL BE EFFECTIVE WHEN USED IN TELEPHONE SELLING

You can skip this section if you already have a company name, have no say in the name you will use, or don't want to bother changing your name.

However, if you do not have a company name, or you have the flexibility to create another corporation, or a division, that you can use as your "telephone selling arm," here are a few factors to keep in mind when selecting the name:

• Avoid names that instantly tip prospects to what you do before you get a chance to capture their interest. "Quantum Productions" sounds impressive but doesn't reveal to people that you are a printer selling color printing services. "Quantum Four-Color Printing and Prepress" does tip your hand early and may cause prospects to say "not interested" prematurely. Suggestion: If your name is already Quantum Four-Color Printing and Prepress and you don't want to change it, give your company name simply as "Quantum" the first time you use it.

• Use a name that is relatively easy to say and easy to remember. "Logistics Associates" is better than "Shaupchaur, Leissam, and Bechquapinskiov Shipping and Transportation Services." If you're stuck with the latter name, consider shortening it to SLB Services when giving your company name over the phone.

• Pick a name that will impress the prospect. Corporate sounding names, names that sound like associations or institutes, and official-sounding names can all make you seem bigger than you are.

• Target the name to your market and the type of business you are in. For instance, let's say your name is Joe Smith and you are a motivational speaker, writer, and publisher. Which name sounds better, Smith Publishing or The Center for Entrepreneurial Success?

• If possible, use a name that can be abbreviated. The Center for Entrepreneurial Success, for example, can be abbreviated to CES after first usage. This saves time when selling over the phone or writing correspondence.

Fax on Demand

When a prospect has an urgent need, the sales literature she requests should be faxed, e-mailed, or sent via overnight mail or courier for faster delivery than regular first-class mail.

Fax on demand takes this a step further. Fax on demand systems allow prospects to dial into a computerized phone system, listen to a selection of available sales materials, and select the materials.

One of the advocates of fax-on-demand technology as a market tool is Dan Poynter of Para Publishing in Santa Barbara, California. For more information on fax on demand, call Para Publishing toll-free at 800-PARA-PUB.

If getting your prospect on the phone with you is an important step in your selling process, as it is with most tellesellers, you may decide against having a fax-on-demand system. The problem with such systems is that the prospects can request the literature they want without ever speaking to a live salesperson. This is convenient for the prospect but interferes with your objective of engaging the prospect in a phone conversation.

Fax-on-demand systems are a fun, fast, labor-saving, and easy-to-use means of fulfilling requests for literature. Unfortunately, fax-on-demand systems don't qualify prospects; they merely transmit the requested sales documents. The downside is getting flooded with requests and sending out a lot of material to people who are just collecting brochures. Even if they're serious prospects, they haven't shared their name and phone number with you, making it difficult to establish the rapport necessary for effective telephone selling. And remember: Your goal is to make sales, not give out sales literature. Fax on demand, like the Internet, is often less effective for the former than for the latter.

Four

Creating a Telephone Selling Plan That Works

A major negative of telephone selling to many people is that it's hard work. You have to sell—every day. With direct mail, you do some work up front, but once the mailer goes out, it's on its own. You sit back and eagerly anticipate the results (or lack thereof).

With telemarketing and telephone selling, you make your contacts one at a time. Each time you want to reach a prospect, you or one of your telesellers must pick up the phone, dial, and pump yourself up for a challenging call.

Many sales trainers call selling a "numbers game." What this means is you can measure your activity, success rates, and rejections, and on the basis of that measurement determine precisely the amount of sales calls you need to make to achieve your objectives.

To maximize your teleselling success, you must understand how these numbers work, know how to measure them, set sales goals, and design teleselling activity to ensure that the goals are achieved.

The purpose of the plan is to determine the number of calls per day needed to achieve your income objective.

Here's an interesting point: Many businesspeople hate telephone selling because they hate being told no. Actually, it doesn't matter if people say no—as they will all the time—as long as (1) a given percentage of the people you call, small though it may be, say yes instead of no, and (2) you call enough people and get enough responses so the total number of yes responses generates the desired sales revenues.

All successful salespeople hear no many times during the day. If you are not hearing no you are not making enough calls and will not achieve your income goal. So don't be afraid of rejection; it goes with the territory.

The "Plan on the Back of an Envelope"

Perhaps you've seen or read books on business or marketing planning and been turned off by them. Some of these planning exercises go too far in terms of length and complexity, to the point where writing the plan becomes more all-consuming than running the business. The plan becomes the end, rather than what it should be: a means to an end.

This is not what I want for you. Planning should take a minimum of time and effort. It should be simple, accurate, and practical. The plan should translate into the precise actions you must do, each day, to achieve your stated objectives.

Let's take a look at how to create a simple but totally effective telephone selling plan. The elements of the plan include:

- Income objective
- Average unit of sale and sales volume
- Conversion rate

- Call volume and prospecting rate
- Calls per day required

This plan is so brief and simple you can literally write it on the back of an envelope (but use a clean sheet of paper anyway), and you can do it in about ten minutes. Have a calculator handy.

Income Objective

How much money do you want to gross this year from telephone sales? Write down the amount on a piece of paper. Now divide by 12 to determine the amount of money you want your telephone sales operation to gross every month. For example, gross annual sales of $100,000 translates into sales of $8,334 per month.

Now divide $100,000 by 50 weeks (assuming you are closed 2 weeks each year) to determine the amount of money you want to gross each week. To gross $100,000 a year, you need to average $2,000 a week. Write all these numbers down.

Average Unit of Sale and Sales Volume

What is the gross amount of your average unit of sale? $100? $1,000? $10,000? Write down this number on your paper.

Divide your total sales goal for the year by the dollar amount of the average unit of sale. This will show you how many sales you have to close to reach your stated objective. For example, if your income objective is $100,000 in sales and your average sale is $5,000, you have to close 20 sales this year to reach your goal.

Conversion Rate

Obviously, your telephone calls will generate inquiries. But not everyone who makes an inquiry will become a customer. In fact, most won't.

The conversion rate is the percentage of leads that will become customers after repeat follow-up efforts are made. If you make one sale for every ten inquiries, your conversion rate is 1:10, or 10 percent. If you convert one out of every four inquiries to a sale, your conversion rate is 1:4, or 25 percent.

Calculate your conversion rate now and write it down on your paper, preferably as a fraction—1/2, 1/3, 1/15 . . . you get the idea.

If you haven't done much teleselling and don't know what your conversion rate is, make an educated guess. Anywhere from 1/10 to 1/3 is typical for many telesellers.

Now, flip the fraction. If your conversion rate was 25 percent, or 1/4, flipping the fraction gives you 4/1, or 4. If your conversion rate was 10 percent, or 1/10, flipping the fraction gives you 10/1, or 10. Flip your fraction and write down the new number.

Now multiply this number times your required sales volume, or number of sales. If your number is 10, and your required sales volume is 20 sales, multiply 10 by 20 and get 200. This is the number of leads you must generate from your telephone selling efforts to meet your sales goal.

This makes sense. You only close 1 prospect out of every 10 leads you generate. Therefore, if you generate 10 inquiries, and close 10 percent, you get one sale. To get 20 sales, you must generate 200 leads. You will close 10 percent, for 20 orders, to give you the 20 sales you need.

Call Volume and Prospecting Rate

Okay. We know you have to get 200 leads to make your sales quota of $100,000, or 20 deals closed. (A "lead" is an inquiry from a potential customer.)

But most calls do not result in a lead. So we have to make many calls to get one lead. How many calls do we have to make to get the required number of leads to achieve our sales quota?

First, determine how many calls you have to make to get one

person to say, "Yes, I might be interested; tell me more." If you get 1 positive response for every 10 calls, with the other 9 calls resulting in hang-ups or rejections, your number is 10: You make 10 calls to produce one lead. If making 20 calls results in one lead—1 yes and 19 no's—your number is 20. If for every 15 calls you make, you find 1 potential customer, your number is 15.

Think about your calling success rate. Write down your number.

Now take this number and multiply it by the number of leads you require to meet your sales goal.

In our example, we have already determined you need 200 leads to make the 20 sales that will result in $100,000 in income. Let's say your new number is 15; you must make 15 calls to get one sales lead. Multiply 200 (leads required) by the number 15, and you find you must make 3,000 calls this year to achieve your objective.

You know the number of leads you need. You know how many calls it takes to generate one lead. Multiply these two numbers. You'll get a large number that tells you how many telephone sales calls you must make this year to achieve your objective. Write the number down.

Calls per Day Required

You will be making telephone sales calls 5 days a week, 50 weeks a year, for a total of 250 days spent on the telephone.

Divide the total number of calls you must make this year by 250. This tells you the most important number in your plan: the number of calls you must make each business day to achieve your sales objective. Calculate this number. Write it down.

You'll be relieved to see how small the number of calls per day is compared to the rather large number of calls per year, which naturally seems intimidating. For example, if you divide

3,000 calls by 250 days, you get 12. Therefore, you must make 12 calls a day to achieve your sales objective of $100,000 in revenue.

SUMMARIZING THE PLAN

Having gone through this planning process, you now have written down on your piece of paper the following information:

Income objective

Average unit of sale

Number of sales to make

Conversion rate

Lead rate

Yearly call volume

Number of calls per day

For our example, the plan should look something like this:

Annual income objective: $100,000

Average unit of sale: $5,000

Number of sales required to meet annual income objective: 20

Conversion rate (percentage of leads that convert into sales): 10 percent

Number of leads required (based on conversion rate) to meet goal: 200

Prospecting rate (number of prospects you must call to produce one good lead): 15

Total number of calls to make this year: 3,000

Sales calls to make each day: 12.

The bottom line of the plan is the last number. You now know what your goal is and exactly what you must do each day to achieve it: Make 12 calls to prospects on your list. What could be simpler?

A Few Important Facts About Your Telephone Sales Plan

1. You need to have a sales goal. If you don't know how much money you want to generate, how do you know whether you're on track?
2. You need to have a "back of the envelope" telephone selling plan. If you don't know how many calls are required each day to achieve your sales objective, how do you know when you've made enough calls for the day?
3. The numbers in the plan are statistical averages. They may vary from day to day. If you don't make your sales quota one day, don't be discouraged. Tomorrow you may get two or three good leads instead of the usual one.
4. Conversely, if you have an extraordinarily good day, that doesn't mean you can coast and not make your calls the next day. Remember, things average out. You will have your good days and bad days. The important thing is to know how many calls the plan requires you to make each day—and then make them, every day.
5. By varying your message and improving your skills, you can improve your prospecting and conversion rates, which will change the numbers. You'll be able to achieve the same sales

volume with fewer calls. Or you can make the same number of calls and generate more sales for the effort.

6. Failure to achieve the objective in telephone selling usually does not come from inadequate prospecting or conversion rates. You know the rates and what you have to do to achieve your sales goal within those rates. Most times, failure is caused by not sticking with the teleselling plan—that is, not making the sales calls, or not making enough sales calls, or not doing them every day. When you make fewer calls than your plan specifies, your leads and closings will go down proportionally.

7. Conversely, if you step up your telephone sales activities, you'll make more calls, talk to more prospects, generate more leads, and close more sales. A good strategy for boosting sales incrementally without a major change in your daily routine is to increase call activity about 10 percent beyond what the plan calls for. For example, if your plan says you should be making 12 calls a day, make 13 or 14 calls. Do this and your sales will increase by 10 to 20 percent.

8. Keep records of all telephone selling activities, including the number of calls made each day, number of people you spoke with, number of leads generated, and sales closed. Records tell you whether what you're doing is working and, if so, how well.

☎ *Five* ☎

Where to Find Good Calling Lists

 This chapter will help you

- Determine the profile of your target market
- Deal more effectively with list vendors and brokers
- Identify the right telephone list
- Effectively test lists before program rollout

What Is a Calling List?

Telemarketing and teleselling success is dependent on your calling list selection—the names and phone numbers of people you will call. But the calling list (usually called a telemarketing list) isn't just the way you *reach* your market; it *is* the market! If you cannot identify and rent appropriate calling lists, your chances of success are poor.

After your offer itself—the product and its price—list selection is the most important factor in determining telephone selling response. For example, an outstanding technique and script might pull double the response of a poorly conceived pitch. But a good calling list can outpull a weak list by two to five times the responses or more.

Approximately thirty thousand different direct-marketing lists are available for rental, representing a combined database of some one billion names. There are few persons in the United States whose names are not on at least one of those lists. All lists have names and addresses; a large percentage have phone numbers. Some also have fax numbers and a few have e-mail addresses.

List Types

The basic categories of available calling lists include the following:

• *House list.* An in-house list usually contains names of customers, people who have bought from you, and prospects, people who have inquired but not bought. House lists are best because they frequently pull double or more the response of even the best-performing rented lists.

• *Compiled lists.* These lists contain names of people or businesses compiled from published sources, such as industry directories and the Yellow Pages. Compiled lists frequently provide the best means of reaching large groups of specific audiences. For example, you can rent compiled lists of all attorneys in New York City or all radiologists in the United States.

• *Response lists.* These are lists of proven mail-order buyers. Mail-order offers usually get the best return from response lists of buyers who have purchased a product similar to yours and in the same price range. For example, a $10 book on small-business success is likely to sell best to people who have bought similar books in the $8 to $15 price range.

• *Attendee/membership/seminar lists.* These lists contain

names of individuals who have attended a specific trade show or industry event, belong to an industry association or professional group, or have paid for seminar participation. Since relatively costly trade show attendance, memberships, and seminars are usually sold through direct marketing, excellent results are possible from such lists.

• *Subscription lists.* These are some of the best and largest lists on the market. Two types of subscription list exist: controlled circulation and paid circulation. With controlled circulation, the readers receive the magazine free, provided they can prove to the publisher that they fall into a certain professional category. For example, to receive a free computer magazine, the reader must work in the data-processing department at a firm of a certain minimum size. Proof consists of a completed subscription request form or "qualification card." With paid circulation, the reader pays for a subscription and is not required to provide additional data other than name and address. Each type has its pros and cons. For mail-order offers, paid-circulation lists may be the better choice, because those on the list have purchased a product—the magazine—through the mail. However, controlled-circulation lists offer the advantage of greater selectability. Because the subscribers have given a lot of information about themselves, you can select portions of the list according to certain characteristics, which might include job title, job function, size of company, or even the types of products purchased.

• *Donor lists.* Used primarily by fund-raisers, these lists contain the names of people who have contributed money to charities and nonprofit organizations.

• *Credit-card holder lists.* The names on these lists are ideal for teleselling because the prospects can respond to your offer using a credit card. Also, credit-card holders are somewhat "upscale," demonstrated by the fact that they earn enough money to qualify for a credit card. These lists are especially good if you want to take orders over the phone, because you know in advance that the prospect has a credit card.

• *Merged database lists.* This type of list simplifies selection because merging lists eliminates duplicate names and offers the remaining names as a single master unduplicated list. One example is the International Thomson Retail Press (ITRP), a master list of 175,737 executives in wholesale, manufacturing, retail, and service industries derived from highly selective qualified trade publication subscriber lists. Such databases allow list users to reach a large portion of a specific market without having to track down obscure, hard-to-find, or poorly managed lists.

List Vendors

Telemarketing lists are usually rented for one-time use. If you want to do a second mailing, you must rent the list again. The names and addresses of people who respond to your original mailing, however, become your property and can be added to your own in-house list.

Lists are generally available from three sources: the list owner, a list manager, or a list broker. A fourth source, of course, is to compile your own lists from appropriate publications.

• *List owners.* Many marketers and private organizations rent their own in-house lists. If you wanted to rent a list of people who attended, say, the Chemical Exposition, you could call the show sponsor and see if the list is available.

• *List managers.* Because the administrative details of list rentals are time-consuming, many list owners hire outside firms, called list managers, to manage and market their lists for them. If a list is handled by a list management firm, you would rent it from that firm rather than the owner. Also, list managers aggressively promote their lists to generate commissions from rentals; many of the ads featuring lists are placed by list management firms.

• *List broker.* A list broker is a third-party agent that acts as liaison between the list owner or manager and the mailing-list user. Unlike list managers, who work primarily for the list owner, list brokers work primarily for you, the list user. Also, while managers have a vested interest in promoting their own lists, brokers can be more objective in their recommendations. All brokers have access to the same lists, but they differ in the service, advice, expertise, and recommendations they offer clients. Approximately 80 percent of all list rentals are made through brokers.

Profiling Your Target Market

A key component of successful teleselling strategy is generating a profile of your target market or "ideal customer," then selecting lists of people who most closely fit this profile. The following selection factors, reflected in many lists, should be kept in mind as you develop your profile:

Geographic

Most lists can be segmented by location: state, SCF (sectional center facility; all zip codes included under a given SCF share the same first three digits), zip code, county, and metropolitan area. If you are planning a phone campaign designed to get businesspeople to attend a conference in New York City, you might phone or mail only to executives located within a hundred-mile radius of midtown Manhattan.

Demographic

Some lists provide quantitative characteristics of a given population: age, sex, income level, wealth, race, and other vital statistics of a personal nature. A great many lists, for instance, allow selection by gender.

Psychographic

This segmentation refers to the psychological makeup of your target audience and is more difficult to identify. A campaign to fill seats for a seminar called "How to Become a Published Author" might be aimed at members of the American Association for Retired Persons, on the assumption that many retirees are looking for something to occupy their time and might consider writing for publication. The premise is unproven, however, and a test mailing to this list might fail to generate sufficient response. A better choice might be the *Writer's Digest* subscription list, where people have indicated their interest in writing by buying a magazine on the subject.

Buying Patterns

Three important selection criteria for mail-order buyers are frequency (how often they buy through the mail), recency (the date of their last purchase), and amount spent. Many list descriptions provide a dollar amount for "average order," representing the average amount spent by people on the list for one order.

Experience shows that buyers who buy often and spend more are better prospects than those who buy infrequently and spend less. Also, contrary to what might seem logical, the persons most likely to respond to a new mail-order offer are those who have recently responded to one! This is why "hotlines," the segment of a list comprising the most recent buyers, are priced higher than the rest of the list.

Business Factors

Business list selection criteria include job function, title, plant size, industry (often specified by Standard Industrial Code), number of employees, annual sales, and types of products purchased.

Market Research as an Aid to List Selection

Market research studies, especially those involving focus groups, can help define an accurate profile of your target prospect, which in turn simplifies the process of selecting the right lists for your offer.

Many telephone marketers use market research to avoid costly errors and to correct misconceptions about their prospect or the perceived benefits of their product. Nonetheless, most agree that no amount of market research can predict a winner or guarantee success. The only accurate measure of selling success is to test a small portion of the list and analyze the return.

Using List Brokers

The best way to find a good list broker is through referral. Call colleagues, associates, and others who rent phone lists and ask for recommendations. You can also find brokers in the Yellow Pages under "Mailing Lists" and ads in such direct-marketing publications as *Direct Marketing, Target Marketing,* and *DM NEWS.*

The broker's key function is to provide timely and informed

recommendations about which lists you should test and why. The broker should provide a detailed report on each recommended list. Be suspicious of brokers who regard your request for more information as an affront or a waste of their time.

In addition to providing list recommendations and information, your broker should handle the administrative aspects of list rental and delivery, follow up on all details, and make sure your lists are delivered by deadline. Brokers do not charge list users for their services but are paid a commission from the list owner or manager; hence, there is no extra fee for renting through a broker instead of going directly to the list owner.

How to Evaluate List Recommendations

Although the mailing list supplier can make recommendations, only you are responsible for making the final decision concerning which lists to test. You can make a better choice by taking the time to study the broker's list recommendations.

Information about a list is traditionally provided in a format known as a data card. This document—a letter-size sheet of paper or a computer printout—contains basic information on the list. For each list, you should look for the following:

• *List size.* Lists range in size from less than two thousand names to one million names or more. The traditional approach is to test a small portion of the list, then mail to a larger portion if the test is successful. Telephone sellers phoning smaller numbers of prospects are happy to find good lists even if the size is limited. Furthermore, to the marketer seeking unusual or hard-to-find prospects, such small specialized lists may be the only means of reaching certain markets.

• *Cost per thousand.* Prices typically range from $75 to $125 per thousand names, with specialized lists going for as much as $150 per thousand and more. Be wary of firms offering so-called "bargain lists" selling for $25, $10, or even $5 per thousand; often these are worthless.

• *List description.* Each data card contains a paragraph or two about the background of the list: its source, history, a profile of the type of buyers it represents, and a description of the product they bought, the publication they subscribe to, or the seminar they attended. Read the description to get a feel for the market represented by the list.

• *Average size of order.* Given as a dollar amount, this represents the average size of the mail-order purchase made by the buyers on the list. Average size of order is a good indication of whether people on this list might be willing to pay your price.

• *Hotline.* As I said, this is a segment of the list that represents "hot" customers who have recently made a mail-order purchase, usually within the last 30 to 90 days (the more recent, the better). Hotlines typically rent for $5 more per thousand than the rest of the list.

• *Active versus inactive, buyer versus prospect.* Customer lists almost always pull better than prospect lists. If you're thinking of testing a list of newsletter subscribers, for example, rent the list of current (active) subscribers rather than the list of former subscribers whose subscriptions have expired. When renting a list from a mail-order catalog company, obtain the names of people who have actually bought from the catalog, not those who merely requested a free catalog but did not buy.

• *List-usage report.* Try to get the list supplier to tell you how well the list pulled for other people who rented it, especially those with offers similar to yours. This information probably won't appear on the data card, but it may be contained in a separate list-usage report available from the broker. List-usage reports usually show rental activity by tests (initial campaigns) and continuations (rental of additional names following a successful test). If a high percentage of the marketers who tested are also listed under continuations, they are getting test results profitable enough to warrant continued use of the list, which means it is working for them.

• *Selections available.* The data card indicates the selection criteria by which the list can be segmented. These can include sex, marital status, age, profession, geography, and credit card status. In general, the more selections, the better, because selectability allows you to sell only to those people who are closest to your target profile. For example, if you are selling infertility treatments, you want to select married couples without children.

• *Frequency of updating.* Question the list's "cleanliness." Are the names current and is the list frequently updated (no-longer-current names are removed)? Approximately one fifth of the population moves every year, so compiled and prospect lists get dated quickly. As a rule, a list should be updated at least once a year.

How to Order Your Lists

Most brokers and managers require a minimum order of five thousand names per list (not per order). By ordering all lists through a single broker, you may be able to get 10–60 percent volume discounts.

Traditionally, brokers are paid only for the actual number of names rented. However, there is a movement in the list industry to create a new payment structure whereby brokers are compensated for the consulting service they provide, not just for the net number of names rented. Do not be surprised if some brokers actually request an up-front retainer for making recommendations. In most cases, this fee will be credited toward list rental, so that the consultation costs you nothing if you buy from the broker who gave you the advice.

Almost all list owners, whether you rent from them directly or through a manager or broker, reserve the right to review your sales script or literature before accepting your list order. Be sure to send two copies of the script or your brochure to your list supplier so this can be taken care of promptly. Although most campaigns are approved, list owners occasionally deny use (especially if your offer is competitive with theirs or if they think it will offend their customers in some way).

When ordering, you must specify the medium on which you wish to receive the names. Telephone lists can be provided in the following formats and media:

- CD-ROM
- Floppy disk
- Magnetic tape
- Computer transmission
- Telemarketing cards (index cards with one prospect file per card)
- Computer printouts
- Notebook or directory form, usually in a three-ring binder

DIRECTORIES

A *prospecting directory* is a printed directory of contacts within a specific industry or market segment. The directory is designed for use as a prospecting list for direct mail and telephone selling. You are given complete contact information and background on each firm listed so that you can effectively reach your target prospect within that organization via mail or phone.

An *industry directory* is a directory of resources, vendors, companies, and other key players within a particular industry. While not designed specifically for prospecting, industry directories often contain most of the same information prospecting directories do. Therefore, many telephone sellers seek out and use directories covering their target industries as prime list sources.

The biggest advantage of directories over rented lists for tele-sellers is the low cost. You can get a good directory containing a database of hundreds or thousands of potential customers for between $50 and $500, depending on the source, and they may be available for free in general or specialized libraries. This compares favorably with list brokers, who charge an average of $100 per thousand names and often have a five thousand–name minimum order. A directory is also a more convenient format than cards or printouts.

The main disadvantage of directories is they can be somewhat out of date. Many rental lists are updated every six or twelve months, so the names are never more than a year old. An annual directory, on the other hand, stays in print for a year. But the directory must first be researched, compiled, typeset, printed, bound, and distributed. And most directory buyers don't buy a new edition every year; they tend to use an old directory for one, two, or three years before buying a new one. The danger is that you risk working with old information.

This is a negative, but not a terrible one. If you are doing direct mail and a mailing list is out of date, the mailer is either undeliverable or reaches the wrong party, and you have wasted the 50 or 60 cents it took to mail the piece. You don't find out where that person went or who has taken her place. The sales contact is not made.

On the other hand, if you are doing telephone sales, and the person you are calling is no longer with the company, you have potentially doubled the number of contacts you can make from that listing. First, you ask who has taken the first person's place, and you speak to this person. You also ask if the company has the new phone number for the employee who has left. Then contact that person at her new company; they may be a prospect for what you are selling.

Finding Good Prospecting and Industry Directories

Finding prospecting and industry directories is not at all difficult. Here's how to uncover the best directories in your market:

1. Pay attention to the direct mail you receive. Directory publishers market their books aggressively and sell mainly through direct mail. Keep a file of mailings promoting directories you think might be of use to you.
2. Consult *Directories in Print* in the reference department of your local library. This is a guide to the directories available to you. You can quickly locate good directories for your target market, industry, or subject area.
3. While you're in the reference room, check out the *Encyclopedia of Associations*. If your prospects belong to one or more trade groups, call these associations and ask whether they have a membership directory. Some will sell you a copy of the directory. Others provide directories to members only. Often you can join the organization as an affiliate member for a small fee and get the directory that way. It's well worth it.
4. Call the publishers of the leading trade journals in your field. Ask if they publish an industry directory and what it costs. Some publishers even give the directory free to subscribers to their journal. Others sell it for a separate price.
5. Your local chamber of commerce probably publishes an annual membership directory. This is useful if yours is a local or regional market. You can also get chamber of commerce directories from municipalities other than your own.
6. Are you a member of a local club, group, or association of busi-

nesses? Many publish small local membership directories that make excellent teleselling lists. Often it's worth the $100 or so to join the group for a year just to receive the directory. I have done this a number of times with good results.

7. Ask your colleagues what directories they use or are listed in. Take a look at the books, and if they look good, buy one and try it.

Selected List Sources

American List Council—908-874-4300

Compilers Plus—800-431-2914

Database America—201-476-2000

Direct Media—203-532-1000

Edith Roman Associates—800-223-2194

Hugo Dunhill—800-811-6013

PCS—800-532-5478

In teleselling, you need to know whom to call and what to say. In this chapter, you learned how to get the names and phone numbers of prospects to call. In the next chapter, I'll show you what to say to get these people to buy.

☎ *Six* ☎

Cold Calls: The Opening Script

A cold call is when you pick up the phone, dial a prospect whose name and number you took from some directory or rented telemarketing list, introduce yourself and your company, and try to get him interested in learning more about what you are selling. This prospect is a person you don't know: he hasn't bought from your company and you have never spoken with him before.

Although earlier I advocated using call guidelines or notes instead of following a rigid script, I do think you should have an opening script if you are going to cold-call. This chapter shows you how to put that script together and deliver it effectively.

What Is an "Opening Script"?

An opening script is a prewritten dialogue for handling the initial 30 to 60 seconds of your cold call.

It's important that you get the call off to a good start, and to do this, you must have a pretty good idea of what you want to say and how to say it. You should write an opening script and practice it many times, until it becomes second nature to you. Later on in the call, you'll be responding intelligently to what the prospect says and how he or she sounds and acts. But at the beginning, you have almost no clues from which to take your lead. That's why, to cold-call with confidence, you must be prepared to carry on the first 30 to 60 seconds of your call with little feedback or participation from the prospect. To be effective, the opening script should tell your prospect the following:

1. Who you are—your name and, if appropriate, title
2. The name of your business
3. The reason you are calling
4. The reason why the prospect should be interested in talking with you—or at least in hearing what you have to say

Do you really need all this? Yes. If you leave out or try to defer giving away the first three items (your name, the company name, the reason for your call), the prospect is likely to resent your evasiveness and become annoyed. People want to know whom they are talking to, and why. You can't get around this. But you can present the information in a way that arouses interest rather than turns people off. If you leave out the fourth item, the prospect will quickly lose interest in and motivation for continuing the conversation, and the call is likely to be ended by the prospect in short order.

Fortunately, these four points don't represent an overload of information, and you can get it all in—smoothly, quickly, and without sounding like a salesperson.

There are an endless variety of opening scripts that achieve these objectives with varying degrees of success. But most of them are variations of one of two basic openings: the benefit statement opening and the prospect need–qualification opening. Although I strongly prefer and almost always use the latter, let's take a look at both of these proven openers.

The Benefit Statement Script

In the benefit statement script, you follow the above guidelines, immediately giving the prospect the four key pieces of information: your name, your company name, the reason for your call, and the reason she should be interested. But you do it with a twist.

The twist is this: In the description of your company and the reason for your call, instead of just saying the company name and what its product or service is, you tell the prospect the *benefit* of what you do—not the actual title, product name, service category, or function. Instead of saying you are a financial planner, you say, "I help people become wealthier and retire earlier." Instead of saying you are a color-catalog printer, you say, "I help companies produce better-looking catalogs while significantly reducing their production lead time and printing costs." Here's an example:

MICHAEL JONES (THE TELESELLER): Mr. Doakes?

PROSPECT: Yes, how can I help you?

MICHAEL: Mr. Doakes, my name is Michael Jones, and I'm a catalog production specialist with Royal Printing. Have you heard of us?

PROSPECT: I don't think so.

MICHAEL: We specialize in helping companies like yours produce quality catalogs at a significantly lower production and printing cost than they are now paying. Mr. Doakes, if I could show you how ABC Company can maintain its high standards of quality in your catalogs while cutting printing costs ten to twenty percent, would you be interested in taking a look?

PROSPECT: Well, how would you do that?

Note in the above script the following:

• Michael gives his title as a catalog production specialist. The title you use in telephone sales calls should not contain the word "sales" in it. When prospects hear "sales" in your title, they rightly assume you are a salesperson trying to sell them something that will cost them money, and they want to get away from you as rapidly as possible.

Use what I call a "value-added" title—a title that describes what you do but positions you as helpful adviser or knowledgeable expert instead of a hard-pressure salesperson. If you sell mutual funds, call yourself a financial consultant. If you sell LAN equipment, call yourself a "LAN specialist." A radio commercial for the Vermont Teddy Bear Company encourages listeners to call 800-829-BEAR and speak with a "certified bear counselor"—a value-added name for a telephone order taker.

While prospects want to avoid salespeople, they are more eager to talk with specialists, consultants, experts, technicians, advisers, managers, and others who may have important information that could be of benefit to them.

• After giving his company name, Michael asked, "Have you heard of us?" This inserts a natural break into the conversation that prevents Michael from giving a too-long monologue at the beginning of the call. It gets prospects involved early. If the prospects haven't heard of you, they appreciate that you're modest enough to realize that and to ask them. If they have, they become comfortable talking to a vendor they perceive as well known. Either way, you win.

• At the close of his opening script, Michael asks the prospect, "If I could show you a way to achieve benefit X, would you be interested?" Prospects are more likely to respond positively if you offer a benefit and ask if they want that benefit. Response will often not be as enthusiastic if you merely say, "Are you interested in buying widgets?"

The benefit statement script is used by numerous telesellers and can be very effective. The advantage is that it presents your offer in terms of customer benefits, not product or service or seller.

The disadvantage is that it can come across as a "sales pitch." And some prospects find it evasive. Their feeling: "If you are a printing broker, just come right out and say it; don't ask me if I want to save money on printing. Of course I do. What kind of idiotic statement is that?"

Also, the benefit you stress in your opening may not be the benefit the customer considers most important in evaluating your type of product or service. For instance, if you offer lower costs, and a particular prospect is more interested in higher quality, then you have already disconnected with him. You're not talking about what really interests him; you're not on the same wavelength. And it's difficult to get back on track, because you've already presented yourself as the low-cost supplier, not the quality supplier. To then say, "Oh, we are also better quality" lacks credibility.

This danger can be avoided by using the prospect need-qualification script. Let's take a look at how it works.

The Prospect Need-Qualification Script

In the benefit statement opening, you tell the prospect, "Here is what you need. Here is the benefit, the advantage we offer that other suppliers don't." But, if that benefit doesn't match the customer's concerns, you are in trouble.

In the prospect need–qualification opening, you ask prospects, "What benefits are you most interested in when evaluating products or services like mine?" The prospects tell you. And then you present your capabilities as favorable to helping the prospects achieve their goals better than what they are now buying.

Here's how Michael Jones might have used the need-qualification opening with Mr. Doakes:

MICHAEL JONES (THE TELESELLER): Is this Mr. Doakes?
PROSPECT: Yes, how can I help you?

MICHAEL: My name is Michael Jones, and I'm a catalog production specialist with Royal Printing. Mr. Doakes, are you still the manager of communications at ABC?

PROSPECT: Yes, I am.

MICHAEL: Are you the person responsible for buying four-color printing for your company?

PROSPECT: Yes.

MICHAEL: May I ask you a question?

PROSPECT: Yes.

MICHAEL: Then let me ask you. . . what would it take for Royal Printing to do color-catalog printing for your firm?

PROSPECT: Well, although cost is always important, we're primarily concerned with quality and reliability.

MICHAEL: [You begin to talk about Royal Printing in terms of quality and reliability, not emphasizing price.]

Some important points to note about this script:

• First, Michael Jones qualified the prospect. He asks if he has reached Mr. Doakes, if Mr. Doakes is still the communications manager, and if he is the person in charge of color-catalog printing.

Had Mr. Doakes said he was in fact not responsible for buying color printing, Jones would then ask him, "Can you tell me who that would be?" He would then end the call with Doakes and phone the other person, noting, "I got your name from Michael Doakes," turning the conversation from a cold call into a referral.

• Second, Michael Jones qualified the need. He learned that ABC still bought color printing and was therefore a prospect for his service. If Mr. Doakes had said, "We do it all in-house and no longer buy color printing outside," Jones would know his chances of making a sale to Doakes were extremely limited.

• Third, Michael Jones, having established that ABC buys his type of service and Doakes is the buyer, asks, "What would it take for us to do business together?" Instead of picking one fact about Royal and presenting it to the customer as a benefit, he has asked, "What benefits are you looking for that we might be able to offer you?" When the prospect answers, Jones knows one of two things: Either Royal can't meet the need and this is not a good prospect, or Royal can meet the need, because Royal's capabilities are compatible with the customer's requirements. Knowing this, and knowing what those requirements are, Jones can then effectively present Royal's capabilities in a way that maximizes the customer's interest in the service.

Direct-marketing expert Sig Rosenblum says, "Don't talk about yourself. Talk about the prospect. The prospect isn't interested in your company, your money woes, your sales quota, your equipment. What the prospect is interested in is himself—his problems, his needs, his fears, his business concerns, his sales, his cash flow, his job security." The prospect need–qualification opening is so effective—and for me, so comfortable—precisely because it puts the focus on the prospect, where it belongs, and not on me, my company, my product, or my service.

Try both the need–qualification and the benefit statement opening scripts, and see which works best for you. Vary the scripts in this chapter to fit your own selling situation. Combine them, or create your own opening (be sure to share it with me!).

Shift Delivery to Accommodate Prospect Mood

When delivering your opening script, you can adjust the delivery to fit the reception the prospect is giving you over the phone:

- If the prospect is interested and open to your message, slow down a bit. Be relaxed, friendly, cordial. Have a real conversation. The prospect is inviting you to do so.

- If the prospect is neutral, proceed on an even keel. Don't get too informal or comfy. But take your time, remain professional, and move things along at a reasonably brisk pace.
- If the prospect seems bored, uninterested, or hostile, and your benefit statement or need-qualification opening doesn't warm her up, you may want to politely end the call and move to the next prospect on your list. The person is probably not going to respond positively. At least not today.
- If the prospect seems pressed for time, ask when would be a good time to call back. Make an appointment to call back on that date and time. Make sure the prospect knows it's an appointment. Write it in your appointment calendar. Then follow up and make the call. If the prospect isn't there when you call, keep trying until you do connect.

ADDITIONAL COLD-CALL TIPS

My colleague, the telemarketing consultant Mary Anne Weinstein, offers these additional tips for tellers making cold calls:

1. Make sure your phone provides a clear sound, is comfortable, sturdy, and easy to use. Touch tone produces your ring in half the time of a rotary phone.
2. Let each call ring no more than six times. If you get a busy signal, move on to the next call. Do not replace the receiver after each call. It's a waste of time.
3. Everything rides on your voice. It's more important than your script. Your voice needs to be warm and friendly and properly pitched: not too loud nor too soft; not too fast nor too slow; not garbled nor slurred. It must sound enthusiastic and sincere.

4. Your script needs to tell your listeners who you are, what you are offering, how it will benefit them, and how, when, and what they need to do to buy your product or service. *Don't expect your delivery to be perfect the first time.* You will need to work with it, making modifications as you go. Keep trying. You will get it right.

5. Your list, too, must be tested and qualified. Once you have done this you are ready to begin. Pick up the phone and start making more money!

6. Get a good night's sleep before any day you have earmarked as a teleselling day. Telesellers take more rejection than most people can stand. "Sleep is nature's soft nurse."

7. Take a break after each hour of work, never skip lunch, and don't work for more than four or five hours a day. After four hours productivity decreases greatly.

8. Here is one last tip: Remember that rejection brings you closer to success. Every new day presents its own challenge for outstanding achievement, for superior performance in our every human endeavor.

☎ *Seven* ☎

Cold Calls:
The Presentation Script

A "presentation script" is the portion of your cold call in which you present your product, service, or proposition to the prospect, describing what you offer and how it fits in with the prospect's needs. The presentation portion of the call immediately follows the opening script as described in the previous chapter.

The call should flow smoothly from opening, or qualifying, the prospect to presenting your sales proposition. Callers should be unaware that you have made an evaluation, deemed them a hot lead, and switched to selling mode.

Many face-to-face sellers will ask prospects, "When can I come in to make my presentation?" Never use the term "presentation" when referring to your conversation with the prospect. If the prospect is busy and you are setting up a follow-up call in which you'll get to your presentation, refer instead to "a time to talk about your requirements and how we can help you" or something like that. "Presentation" is a turnoff that says to the prospect, "I want to try to sell you something" rather than, "I want to help you solve your problem."

Although there are as many different sales pitches as there are tellers, most sales presentations fall into one of these four basic categories:

1. Benefit/advantage
2. Survey/question (fact finding)
3. Dialogue/back-and-forth (rapport building)
4. Direct

Let's take a look at each and see how to put them together for maximum effectiveness.

BENEFIT/ADVANTAGE

Since traditional selling is based on appealing to the prospect's desire to gain reward, salespeople are taught, "Stress the benefits of what you are selling, not the features." In other words, don't sell insurance; sell financial security and protection from financial disaster. Don't sell a home computer; sell the importance to parents of having their kids learn the computer early so they get an edge in school and don't fall behind.

In benefit/advantage teleselling, the teleseller rarely mentions the product feature or fact without tying a benefit to it. Therefore, instead of saying, "The X-900 is the most compact copier in our home office line," you would say, "The X-900 is the most compact copier in our line, which means it's ideal for home offices with limited space."

Why does your prospect want to buy your product? What advantages does it offer her? What problems does it solve? How is it superior to and different from other solutions the prospect could buy? Write down these key benefits and advantages. Work them into your presentation script or call guidelines.

Which benefits should you stress? First emphasize the benefits most important to the prospect. Then emphasize the benefits that are unique to your product and service—advantages your competition does not offer. Also, emphasize benefits your competitor offers but does not stress.

But be careful not to overdo it. Use benefit/advantage selling selectively. Don't attach a benefit to every single statement you make. If you do, you'll sound like a salesperson making a pitch—which isn't what you want. Speak naturally. If something rings phony to you, don't say it just because you think you must add a benefit. If you come on too hard, too much like a "salesperson," you risk turning the prospect off.

SURVEY/QUESTION (FACT FINDING)

In this technique you ask prospects questions to find out what they're interested in. Then you present the features and benefits of your product that address the prospects' concerns, interests, needs, wants, and desires.

For instance, if you are selling copiers, you probably can offer many different models with a wide range of features. Which features do you stress? Which model do you try to sell the customer? When you ask questions, the prospect's answers enable you to home in on exactly the right model of copier and to talk about only the features of concern to him.

Often prospects will challenge you with a statement like "We already have a supplier and we are happy with them. Why should we buy from you?"

Instead of going on the defensive, go along with this attitude. Say something like "Maybe you shouldn't" or "I don't know," followed immediately by the probing request, "Tell me what you are looking for." This gives the impression you are interested in making the sale only if your product or service is an ideal fit with the prospect's requirements. The prospect sees you care about helping him, not just filling your bank account with his money. And the prospect also tells you what he needs, so if your product fits, you can present its benefits and features accordingly.

PROSPECT: We might need a new copier. But why should we buy from you?

YOU: I don't know that you should. What are you looking for in a copier?

PROSPECT: One thing our old copier doesn't have that I'd love to have is collating. But we can't afford a big fancy collator.

YOU: Our X-900 CopyMaster might fit the bill. It's one of the only home office copiers with a high-speed, high-capacity collator. The collator is included as part of the machine at no extra cost. And the fourteen-hundred-dollar price is well within the budget we discussed earlier.

Many tellesellers make the mistake of making a "blind" sales pitch: They talk incessantly about products, models, and features without really knowing what the customer is looking for or what will get her excited and interested.

The most successful tellesellers find out what the customer wants, then provide it to her. To find out what the customer wants, just ask. The telephone is an ideal medium for asking questions because you can get an immediate response and reply in context in the next instant. If the prospect says she needs a copier that can reduce large pages to letter size, you immediately focus on the models with that feature, stressing their convenience, simplicity, and low cost.

Be an active listener. Most people who sell do it absolutely wrong. They go in and tell the prospect what they want to say, reciting a memorized list of product features and benefits. But how do you find out what prospects want or desire? First and foremost, you listen. Prospects who do not hear from you what they want to hear from you will tell you so. Often these statements are in the form of objections.

You may think, "I always listen to prospects and clients." But do you? Be honest. Aren't there times when the prospect is talking where you're not really listening but instead planning what you want to say next? And when a prospect says something that you don't agree with or don't want to hear, aren't you immediately planning your rebuttal rather than sitting back and listening to see whether the complaint or statement has merit?

When prospects speak, give them 100 percent of your concentration. Tellesellers, since they can't be seen by prospects, are prone to do other things while they tellesell, which is a mistake. If you're talking with a prospect over the phone, don't go through your mail or write a memo to another customer at the same time. Listening is an active process, not a passive one, and it requires your full attention.

When you talk with prospects, take notes. Jot questions as they occur to you so you don't forget to ask them later on. You can quickly and easily prepare a good proposal or follow-up letter based on detailed notes. When you take notes, your follow-up documents will be full of specific material prospects want to see, because you recorded their requests and preferences.

While the prospect is talking, say things that indicate you are listening and have empathy for what is being said. One simple, effective communication technique for demonstrating your understanding is simply to say "I understand":

PROSPECT: We're looking for a Web site designer who can handle the job from start to finish. I don't want to have to coordinate and deal with half a dozen or more different vendors. We want one firm to do the whole job.
YOU: I understand.

Another technique is to rephrase the prospect's statement and repeat it back:

PROSPECT: We're looking for a Web site designer who can handle the job from start to finish. I don't want to have to coordinate and deal with half a dozen or more different vendors. We want one firm to do the whole job.

YOU: So what you're saying is you want an Internet consultant who can provide all the pieces and provide single source responsibility for getting your home page designed, programmed, written, and put up on the World Wide Web.

PROSPECT: Yes, that's correct.

Equally effective is to rephrase the prospect's statement and repeat it back as a question to which he or she will answer affirmatively. This gets the prospect agreeing to things you say, which eventually leads to a close:

PROSPECT: We really need a Web site that not only disseminates product information but also enables our customers to place credit-card orders directly over the Internet.

YOU: So would you be interested specifically in dealing with a Web consultant with expertise in CyberCash, NetScape Commerce Service, and other means for customers to place orders directly over your Web site?

PROSPECT: Yes, that's what we're looking for.

Some salespeople are more aggressive, phrasing their question so that the answer indicates a tentative (if small) commitment on the part of the prospect:

PROSPECT: We would need video disks to train one hundred IS (Information Systems) staff members in Internet security no later than February 1.

YOU: So if we could provide courseware to train your total staff of one hundred by the first of February, you'd be interested in going ahead?

Why is the survey mode so effective in selling? Because questions demonstrate your concern for the prospect's problems. Asking questions puts the focus of the phone call where it should be: on the prospect's needs, not your products, services, or company.

The survey mode enables you to determine the prospect's requirements so you can tailor your discussion of products and services to address those requirements. In the first call to prospective clients, focus on what they really need to make their problem go away. Don't waste the prospects' time providing a verbal résumé. If prospects need information on your skills, abilities, and experience, they will certainly ask.

Here are some other questions you may find helpful in getting prospects to open up and tell you how you can help them:

"How can I help you?"

"Tell me a little bit about your current situation."

"What specifically do you need me to do for you?"

"What are you looking to accomplish in [their specific area of interest]?"

"That's interesting. Tell me more."

"What are you looking for?"

"What [size/model/capabilities/options/features/accessories] do you consider important in making your purchasing decision?"

"What's the most important factor for you in making this decision?"

Of course, the point of the call is not to ask endless questions or gather infinite information. Each question is designed to clarify and diagnose the prospect's requirements, so that you get as quickly as possible to the point where you can outline your proposed plan of action and your fee.

One variation of the survey/question mode is to design the call so that it is an actual survey. You can tell prospects your company is conducting research to better serve their needs and you want their input on designing new products or tailoring your offering. You can switch to a selling mode with any prospects who have immediate interest in what you are describing. Having done a survey, you have an accurate understanding of their needs, and can position your product accordingly.

DIALOGUE/BACK-AND-FORTH (RAPPORT BUILDING)

Like it or not, personal chemistry is a major factor determining whether prospects buy from you. It's really quite simple: People buy from people whom they like and feel comfortable with. They avoid doing business with people whom they dislike or are afraid of, or who make them uncomfortable.

In certain instances, there will be a strong negative reaction between two personalities that cannot be avoided or controlled. One person will, for myriad reasons, take an instant and overwhelming dislike to another person.

But in most cases you can create good chemistry—or at least create behavior that allows good chemistry to grow and flourish. For instance, if you have a big ego, be aware that most people don't like braggarts and egomaniacs, no matter how smart, right, or good they may be.

In general, people like people who

- Are friendly
- Are warm
- Are courteous
- Are polite
- Are on time
- Are respectful
- Like them
- Share their interests
- Listen to them
- Show an interest in them
- Ask them about themselves
- Treat them well
- Help them

Don't try to force rapport, but if a spark of rapport exists, nurture it, fan it, let it kindle into a warm flame. Your ability to do this depends on whether you are a "people person." If you genuinely like and get along with people, you can probably use this technique with success. If you are aloof and introverted, you'll probably be more successful with the other methods discussed in this chapter.

The key to rapport building is making a one-on-one connection with prospects on a personal level. Often, prospects will make comments of a more personal or general nature during what are otherwise strictly business phone calls. If you have some common ground, let the prospect know it.

For instance, if he comments on last night's game and you are a sports fan, talk about it enthusiastically. Whenever I have a prospect who is working at home and I hear children in the background, I ask the ages and whether they are boys or girls. This is because I love children, and having two young children of my own gives me and the prospect something in common.

DIRECT

In the direct sales mode, you spend most of your time qualifying the prospect, selling benefits, and pushing toward a close. Aggressive financial services sellers promoting stocks over the phone often take this no-nonsense tack.

The advantage is that it can be refreshingly honest. Once a teleseller told me: "Let's not kid ourselves, I'm calling to sell you something. But what I am selling is good for you, and if you give me four minutes, I will tell you why and prove it is so."

The disadvantage is the consumer's natural aversion to tellers, telemarketers, and all other types of salespeople. When you are direct and make it clear you are selling something, many prospects decide immediately they don't want to talk to you. That's a shame if in fact they could benefit from the product you are selling. Had you engaged them about their needs (survey mode), or established a connection on a personal level (rapport-building mode), your chances of getting to talk to the prospects about how you can help them would have been improved.

One question that arises is: How honest should you be about your products and the results you expect to achieve for the prospects? The position I advise you to take is this: Present yourself and your products in the most favorable light possible without misrepresenting yourself.

Naturally, don't make any commitments or claims you can't live up to. But at the same time, remember that your competitors are puffing their own abilities and making themselves look good. They stretch the truth, exaggerate. Some even just plain lie.

You should not lie or exaggerate, but in the face of all this hype, it doesn't pay to be overly modest, either. Present yourself as about 10 percent better than you typically are, as the very best you can be and have been.

Tell all the good things about your product line. Highlight your successes. Don't go out of your way to tell prospects about your weaknesses and failures. Your competitors will gladly do that for you. Present yourself in the most favorable light possible while maintaining complete honesty and integrity. Prospects want to hire people who are successful, not mediocre. Position yourself as such.

When going for the close, use a "preference sell" with a limited range of options or choices. In a preference sell, you do not ask the prospect, "Do you want a hair replacement system?"—a close that risks a "no" answer. Instead, ask the prospect to tell you his preference: "Do you want the Poly-Fuse hair replacement system or would you prefer the Poly-Fix?" Notice that "no" is not a logical answer to this question.

Giving your prospects too many choices either confuses them, if they are the decision makers, or slows down the process if lots of people have to be involved in the decision. Remember, they are looking to you for guidance. If they seem unsure, say, "We could do it this way or this way. Which do you prefer?" By all means, give prospects choices. Prospects resent being told what to do and like to think it was their decision. But in reality, you control the presentation, offering enough options to enable choice without causing confusion.

Another key ingredient in the direct-sales approach (or any of the other presentation modes discussed in this chapter) is enthusiasm. You must be genuinely enthusiastic about your product and what it can do for the prospects. If you are indifferent, disdainful, or even just plain bored, you are unlikely to close the deal.

How do you show enthusiasm? For once, there's no technique for you to learn, because if you are enthusiastic, it will naturally show through in your voice, attitude, manner, and presentation. By the same token, any lack of enthusiasm will also become apparent to the prospect. Just be yourself.

Many novice tellers stumble painfully through sales presentations because they haven't planned in advance what they are going to say. Planning means not only having a well-practiced presentation, but also knowing what to say in reply to prospect comments, questions, and objections.

The key to being polished and smooth is to anticipate what prospects will say and prepare sensible answers in advance. This way, when prospects say "But I can get it cheaper from the printer around the corner," instead of saying "Uhh ... well ... ummm," you launch immediately into a confident, clear explanation of why you should print the brochure even though you cost a bit more.

When you are prepared, you feel confident speaking with prospects and clients. When you are not prepared, you are nervous, because you're afraid they'll state an objection or ask a question to which you have no answer. The more prepared you are, the less likely this is to occur.

The ideal in telephone selling is to be so well prepared that prospects never ask you a question to which you don't know the answer. That's why it's so important, as we discuss in the next chapter, to anticipate objections prospects might raise and know in advance how you will answer them.

☎ *Eight* ☎

Cold Calls: The Objection Script

In teleseling, an *objection* is a reason given by prospects why they are not ready to buy your product or service. For example, if you sell magazine subscriptions, and a potential buyer tells you, "I'm not sure whether I want to get another magazine," that's an objection. The prospect is telling you, "I'm not ready to buy what you are selling, and here's why."

Many tellers fear objections, because these objections get in the way of a quick sale. But the most difficult objection to deal with is the one you do not hear. Let me explain. I fear *not* hearing objections, because chances are the prospects have objections, but they are just not bothering to tell me. And if I don't know about the objections in their heads, I will never get the opportunity to address and overcome them.

Occasionally prospects will not tell you their objections, even though they have them. To make the sale, you must get them to voice their objections and bring them out in the open, where you can deal with them effectively.

The best technique is the "Good, bad, or terrible?" technique developed by my colleagues Fred Weiss and Ken Paston, of

Studebaker-Worthington Leasing. The basic premise is: Whenever you say something to which the prospect does not respond or responds noncommittally, you should proactively get her to react and respond with specifics, so you know whether the sale is on track or whether an objection is threatening to derail you. For example:

> YOU: The total system price comes to $17,500.
> PROSPECT: Uh-huh.
> YOU: How does that sound—good, bad, or terrible?

> YOU: We can finish building the machine, test it out, and assemble, install, and certify it in your plant by the end of October.
> PROSPECT: Okay.
> YOU: How does that sound—good, bad, or terrible?

If the prospect's answer is "Good," you know the terms you proposed are acceptable and the prospect does not object to the deal.

If the prospect answers, "Bad" or "Terrible," ask her, "What's bad about it?" or "What don't you like about it?" She'll tell you her specific objection, which you can then address in your response.

Overcoming Price Objections

Of all the objections, "Your price is too high" is the most common and by far the most difficult to handle.

Here are some techniques that can work for you:

Quote the Price in Terms that Avoid "Sticker Shock."

If your price sounds too high, rephrase so it sounds less costly. Instead of $60, offer three easy monthly payments of $19.95

each. Instead of $100, sell it for $99.95. Instead of $22, make it $19 plus $3 shipping and handling. Instead of $1,000, make it $500 upon order and $500 upon delivery.

Look at the collectibles ads in the Sunday magazine *Parade*. Very few people would agree to buy a Civil War chess set for hundreds of dollars. So the manufacturer sells it to you one piece at a time. While paying $575 for a chess set seems outrageous and would turn customers off, most of us can handle $17.50 for a "hand-painted solid brass knight, modeled after the Civil War cavalry officer."

Offer Leasing or Other Easy Payment Plans.

If you sell an expensive product, system, or service, you know that customers often react with shock when you quote the price. Leasing and other forms of financing allow you to quote the price in terms that sound more attractive. After all, which sounds better to you—"Fifteen hundred dollars" or "Three hundred fifty dollars a month"?

"My standard price quote includes monthly leasing," says a Massachusetts-based computer reseller. "This gives prospects an option which makes our system look less expensive. If the prospects didn't have the lower number to consider, the high purchase price might have blown them away right off the bat. It's a nice selling point, when you are talking to somebody and they start choking on a fifteen-grand price, to say, 'We'll just do the lease for $350 a month.' It tends to get them out of that price-shock mind-set."

Offering financing in-house is convenient to your customers. "By offering leasing in-house, we are giving our customers an extra service which they appreciate," says a small-business owner in Watertown, New York. "If they see you are willing to help them finance the purchase, they are more inclined to buy your product."

Also, if you make customers go outside to look for financing, that gives them more time to change their mind. Offering financing in-house lets you close the deal on the spot.

Financing isn't just for customers who "don't have the money." The traditional perception of leasing and loans is that they appeal only to customers who do not have the money to buy your product outright. But many customers, even those with money, appreciate knowing financing is available from you as an option.

Take corporate customers, for example. Many big companies have plenty of cash. But they finance, lease, rent, or outsource anyway! Reason: The person who wants the equipment may not have the authority to make a large purchase without having it approved by a committee or referring it to the home office. With leasing, they can convert the large purchase to a recurring monthly expenditure that falls within their own operating budget.

Customers with cash may also choose leasing because of the rapid pace of technology change. They hesitate to buy a computer system, because the technology will soon be upgraded, making the system obsolete. By leasing, your customer avoids obsolescence. At the end of the lease, the customer returns the equipment to the leasing company. Incidentally, this creates a built-in second sale for you, since the customer will need to upgrade to a newer system.

Leasing gives you pricing flexibility. By structuring the financing, you can tailor the monthly lease payment to meet the prospect's budget. This enables you to have price flexibility without actually lowering the cost of the product.

Offering leasing as a financing option may help you make the sale even in cases where the customer ultimately decides to buy instead of lease. One office automation dealer says, "I quote monthly lease payments and the purchase price in every situation, because the low monthly payment says to the customer,

'There's a less expensive way to acquire this equipment, if the purchase price is too high.' This keeps them at the table, while quoting only the high purchase price initially might have caused them to walk away."

Find Out the Budget First, Then Tailor the Price to Fit the Budget.

Your best chance of making the sale is if your price quotation is within the prospect's budget. Your best chance of having that happen is to know the budget before you give your price. And the best way of knowing that is simply to ask the prospect what the budget is. Here's a comfortable, nonaggressive way to get this information:

YOU: Do you have a budget?
PROSPECT: Yes.
YOU: Can you give me an idea of what it is?

If the prospect does not have a budget, this conversation might go as follows:

YOU: Do you have a budget?
PROSPECT: No.
YOU: Well, did you have a dollar figure or range in mind of what you'd like it to cost?

About half the prospects will give you an answer so you can tailor your price quote accordingly. The other half won't, so you just have to go ahead and make your estimate without this knowledge.

Stress Cost of Ownership Versus Cost of Purchase.

The purchase price is not the only cost of owning something. There is the cost of maintenance, support, repair, refurbishment, operation, and, when something wears out, replacement. Therefore the product that costs the least to buy may not actually cost the least to own; often it is the most expensive to own!

Example: Several companies are now selling artificial bone substitutes for orthopedic surgeons to use in bone graft operations. As of this writing, a small container of the artificial bone substitute, containing enough material for one spine surgery, can cost $500 to $800.

The shortsighted buyer sees this as expensive, especially since bone graft can be taken from other sites in the patient's own body, and there is no cost for this material.

But is there really no cost? Collecting bone graft from the patient's own body adds about an hour to the surgical procedure. With operating room time at about $1,000 an hour, it makes sense to pay $750 for bone material and eliminate this extra hour in the OR.

That's not all. Often removing the bone from a donor site causes problems that can result in an extra day's stay in the hospital. That's another $1,000 down the tubes. And the removal of bone from the donor site can cause infection, which must be treated with costly antibiotics. Also, the removal process can cause pain; how do you measure the cost of the patient's added suffering? So while $750 for a small vial of artificial bone may seem initially expensive, it is in fact a bargain when compared with the alternative, which superficially appears to have zero cost.

If your product costs slightly more up front but actually saves money in the long run, stress this in your sales talk. Everyone knows that the cheapest product is not automatically the best buy; corporate buyers are becoming especially concerned with this cost-of-ownership concept. Only government business, which is awarded on the basis of sealed proposals and bids, seems still to focus solely on the lowest price. And even that is slowly changing.

Create an Apples-to-Oranges Comparison.

When the prospect can compare two items and find them exactly identical, the price becomes the deciding factor, and the low-priced bidder wins.

Fortunately for tellers and others who do sales, products and services are rarely identical. Multiple differences, some major, some minor, make it virtually impossible to price-compare a large percentage of goods and services with an apples-to-apples comparison. As soon as doing such a comparison is made impossible, you can counteract price objections by pointing out the differences (advantages) of your offer compared to the competition's.

Sometimes these differences are tangible and measurable; sometimes they are intangible. Either type of difference can be sufficient ammunition to destroy apples-to-apples price-comparison resistance.

Say you are selling Internet access services over the phone to consumers. Your price is $19.95 a month. The prospect says, "I can get the same thing from local access provider X for only $18.95 a month." The lower price is attractive because the prospect sees no difference between your Internet access services and those of your competition—she is making an apples-to-apples comparison.

You want to add a factor to the equation that throws this comparison off balance and makes it impossible. "Yes," you say, "but we are the only local access provider that provides telephone support from a live Internet technician twenty-four hours a day, seven days a week. So if you have a problem getting onto the Internet or using the service, we can help you immediately." Now your service is no longer exactly the same as the competition's. An apples-to-apples comparison is impossible—there's no way to adjust price to reflect the added offer of round-the-clock support. So the $1 cheaper price of the competition as an objection disappears.

Scale It Back.

Many people want to buy things they cannot afford. Tele-sellers who represent a product line rather than a single product can accommodate the monetary limitations of prospects by rec-ommending a less expensive item.

When your initial offer is too rich for the prospect, scale it back. For example, if the prospect can't afford the 1,200 dpi laser printer, suggest they get the 300 dpi printer. It's almost as good, and it fits his or her budget. If they can't afford a color laser printer but need color output, show them a more affordable color inkjet printer.

Prospects with limited funds—and that's almost everyone you call—understand that they can't have everything they want or the top-of-the-line model with all the accessories all the time. This is true even in the funeral business. Nobody really *needs* a $4,000 coffin (the deceased doesn't care), so if the family is on a limited budget, they can still have a lovely funeral but keep within their budget by scaling back to a $2,500 or $2,000 casket.

Use a Differentiator.

A *differentiator* is a quality or feature that differentiates your product or service from the competition's. The key is to make prospects understand that, although two products may be virtu-ally identical, no two are supported by the supplier in exactly the same way. It is the differences between the way you render after-sale support and services versus the competitor's operation that enables you to say to prospects, "The slightly higher prices we charge are a drop in the bucket compared with the quality and results you get." Of course, you must back up such an assertion with details and proof.

Here are some examples of effective differentiators that have been used with success:

- Guaranteed performance/quality
- Extra service or free service

- Extended warranty
- Free delivery or shipping
- Free installation
- Free model upgrade (e.g., from a compact to a midsize rental car)
- Free rebate or cash bonus
- Discount for payment with order
- Free training
- Free maintenance or touch-up
- Free gifts
- Free trial
- Expanded choice of colors, sizes, models, options, or accessories

Target Value-Conscious Buyers.
Despite all these methods, you will lose some sales simply because these techniques do not work with certain types of buyers. There are some people for whom price is the be-all and end-all, either because they truly believe low price means the best value, or because they have so little money.

Fortunately, a large number of prospects do not buy solely on price. Most of them instead want to make sure they are getting the most value for their money. They will pay a higher price if they feel they are getting a superior solution.

After a while, tellesellers can quickly identify who is a value buyer and who is a price buyer. The trick, then, is to simply avoid selling to price buyers, unless your competitive advantage happens to be that you offer the lowest price. Don't try to convince someone who always picks the lowest-priced product they shouldn't do so. Instead, target value buyers. Focus the conversation on demonstrating to them that you offer the best value. As the saying goes: Preach to the converted.

How do you demonstrate the superior value of your product without sounding as though you're boasting? When you say, "We give more value for the money," how do you prove it? The prospects tend to reject such claims, precisely because they come from you, and you are not a neutral party.

In an article in *Small Business Computing*, sales trainer Barry J. Farber recommends that you let your satisfied customers do your selling for you by serving as references and providing testimonials. "If a prospect objects to your rates, say, 'I'd like our client Mr. Jones to call you. He's been paying a little more for our service, and he'll tell you how the long-term benefits have reduced his costs,' " advises Farber.

Make Sure the Price Is Within Their Budget or What They Want to Pay.

"Your fees are too high" can mean "We have the money to do this work, but we're not convinced your service is worth the price you are asking." The objection "We don't have the budget" lays the blame on the buyer, not the seller. It says, "Your fee is perfectly reasonable, but it is not within our budget." Or to put it in more basic terms: "We're too poor."

How do you handle this? It depends on what the true situation is.

In some cases, they *do* have the budget, and are just hoping that by giving this objection, you'll come down in price. When you stick by your original estimate and give reasons why your service is worth the money, you'll find that prospects who said they had no budget can somehow, somewhere come up with the funds to retain you.

At other times, they may honestly not have the cash or have a budget allocated to handle your fees. You then say, "Fine. Tell me what your budget is, and we'll see what we can do for you within that price range."

When they tell you their budget, you don't cut your price to fit that budget. Instead, you offer them a less costly alternative— a more "bare bones" service that's in line with what they can afford.

For instance, say a small business wants a computer system you sell, but when you quote the price of $4,500, the owner says, "That's more than I can afford." When you question him, you discover he wanted to spend around $3,500 but would be willing to go as high as $4,000 for the right system. You tell him, "We can give you the system for $4,000 if we substitute a Brand X color printer for the Brand Y color printer we quoted." If you can assure the buyer that the Brand Y printer is not inferior and will be more than adequate for their needs, you stand a good chance of getting the order.

The idea is to give them the product that fits their budget. If they want the top-of-the-line Brand X printer, they're going to have to pay full price for it. If your price for a premium system is $4,500, don't drop the price just because customers plead poverty. Instead, if their budget is only $4,000, sell them the system they can buy for that amount.

Remind Prospects that Cheaper Is Not Always Better.

"Most prospects know that you get what you pay for, and that the cheapest price is not necessarily the best price," says marketing consultant Ilise Benun. "They just tend to forget it sometimes or hope that it won't hold true when they are making their current buying decision."

Therefore, reminding prospects that cheaper is not better can be an effective tactic in preventing them from buying on price only or on price primarily. Here prospects are not telling you they can't afford you or that you are not worth your fee. They're simply noting that your competitor sells a similar product (they think) over the phone for less, and why should they pay you $1,000 when they can get the same thing from Company X for only $800?

It's basic to human nature: We all want to get the best and pay the least. Unfortunately, the laws of supply and demand say that excellence costs. And deep down we know that the best product or service is rarely the one with the lowest price.

So remind prospects of this. They want the best, so the fact that they can get it cheaper elsewhere is really beside the point, isn't it? Everyone is familiar with the saying "You get what you pay for." Most of us know it's true; we just try not to think of this fact when our budget is limited and we are price-shopping. Remind them, in your own words, of what they already know and believe: You get what you pay for. The lowest price is not necessarily the best price.

One way to do this without being offensive is to help prospects recall a time when they bought on price only and were later sorry they did:

PROSPECT: I am talking to someone locally who can do the job for a lot less money.
YOU: I understand. But let me ask: Have you ever in the past chosen someone because his price was the lowest, only to be disappointed once the job was done?

Another effective technique is to ask prospects point-blank whether they are price shoppers (some people are).

PROSPECT: I am talking to someone locally who can do the job for a lot less money.
YOU: Let me ask . . . are you primarily concerned with price—or with reliability, service, quality [or whatever advantage you offer]?

Most prospects will insist that they want quality, service, or some other advantage you offer. You must then offer proof that you can deliver these benefits and get prospects to agree that superior quality and service quite naturally cost a bit more, but the results are worth it.

A few prospects will tell you, "I buy primarily on price" or "It's a competitive bid situation." Unless you feel certain your price will be the lowest, don't bother pursuing such prospects. Say, "I understand. Some people prefer to buy primarily on price, and my product is not for them. But do call me when you have a job that needs my special touch and you have a budget that will allow us to work together. I'm looking forward to it!"

Point out to prospects that it's cheaper to hire you now and get the job done right than to hire an inferior service, pay the fee, then pay you again to correct their mistakes.

> PROSPECT: I am talking to someone locally who can do the job for a lot less money.
>
> YOU: I spend a lot of time getting paid to correct the work of vendors who do not have the expertise or training to do this type of work correctly. Surely it would be less expensive to have the job done right the first time, rather than pay for an inferior job from an unqualified source now, then pay me to fix it later on. Do you agree?

Compare your credentials, track record, results achieved for customers, and other qualifications with the competing firms'. If you have a strong record of proven success and a long list of satisfied customers, stress these. Customers will pay extra if they have more confidence in your ability to get the job done reliably and on time.

How to Answer the Prospect Who Says, "My Boss/Committee/Spouse Has to Approve It"

"It looks good to me, but of course I don't have the authority to give you the go-ahead; I'll need to run it by my boss/committee/family for approval."

You can avoid this objection by making sure you talk only (or primarily) to decision makers, not to underlings.

Knowing who the decision maker is for your type of service helps put you in front of the right people. If you normally deal with IS managers when selling your consulting services, and you are talking to someone with the title administrative coordinator, you know you're dealing with an underling and must make an effort to present your pitch to the *real* buyer.

HOW TO OVERCOME PROSPECTS' FEARS THAT YOU MAY NOT BE ABLE TO SATISFY THEM

To combat this objection, offer a strong warranty, guarantee, pledge of satisfaction, or promise of performance—within reasonable limits, of course. For example, say something like the following:

"Use the equipment in your factory for a full month. If it does not at least double your manufacturing throughput while reducing raw material costs ten percent or more, let us know. We will send a truck, pack up and remove the equipment, and tear up your purchase order—you will owe us nothing."

"Most of my customers are pleased and satisfied with our Web sites when they review them. But if you are not, I will redesign your Web pages according to your instructions and at my expense."

"We do not consider the job done until the customer is satisfied. We send a bill only when you say we have earned our fee."

"We offer an unconditional one-year warranty on parts and labor, with on-site technical service and support available twenty-four hours a day, seven days a week, even on weekends and holidays."

If you cannot guarantee results, at least promise the prospect your best effort:

"We have been retained by more than forty firms, and in every case, sales have gone up after the customer retained us. While we cannot guarantee the same result for you, we will do our best to achieve it."

Guarantees are powerful incentives for people to do business with you. The longer the terms (ninety days versus thirty days, one year versus three months) and the fewer conditions (an unconditional money-back guarantee is most powerful), the less reluctant prospects will be to do business with you.

A good guide to structuring a successful guarantee is to study the guarantees offered by your competitors, then construct yours so that it is *slightly* better than theirs but not dramatically so. You want enough difference so that your guarantee becomes a strong competitive selling point without locking you into promises you can't afford to make or don't want to keep later.

For instance, if your main competitor in the computer repair business offers a one-year warranty on labor and ninety days on parts, you should advertise a one-year unconditional warranty on labor *and* parts. Then stress your superior guarantee in your sales pitch.

PRACTICE YOUR OWN OBJECTION/ANSWER SCENARIOS

We have just reviewed a few of the most common objections, with strategies for overcoming them. I'm sure you'll encounter many more objections as you make sales presentations to potential customers. When you do, write them down, noting what you said to the prospect and vice versa.

Study the most common objections, the ones that you hear again and again. Write out scripts to answer them, and go over them until they're ingrained in your memory.

Try these scripts out on your next phone calls. If they work, fine. If not, rewrite and adjust until you find just the right words for overcoming the objection.

The key to overcoming objections successfully is preparation. Ideally, you should never hear an objection to which you don't already know the answer. When you know what to say to convince prospects their objections aren't a good enough reason not to buy from you, the objections won't work.

Only when you don't have a good answer can prospects use objections effectively as an excuse not to do business with you. And that's all most objections really are—excuses prospects use to avoid taking action or making a decision.

Keep in mind that every prospect is different. A benefit that is meaningful to one buyer may be unimportant to the other. You must find out what's important to the prospect you're on the phone with and then address that concern.

Even when the facts support your case, you won't always get the sale. Every prospect brings different prejudices to the table. You cannot please or sell everyone. You shouldn't even try. For most of us, we'll make a nice living selling one prospect in ten. If we sell three in ten, we will earn a huge amount of money. So why do you get depressed when you call ten people, and eight do not buy? Be realistic.

☎ *Nine* ☎

Getting Past the Secretary: The Challenge of Selling to Businesses

Those of you who sell to businesses have a problem that consumer service marketers do not: namely, getting past the secretary, receptionist, or assistant when calling to speak with the prospect. "I refer to secretaries and receptionists as 'filters' because they were hired to filter calls," says sales trainer Bill Bishop. "Some calls are to be filtered through, and some are to be filtered out."

This chapter presents proven strategies for handling secretaries so that they are not offended by your tactics—but so you also get through to the person you want to speak to.

TIMING OF PROSPECT CALLS

One way to get past the secretary is simply to call at a time when the prospect is likely to be in, but the secretary isn't. Many secretaries work standard office hours, while some hard-driving business executives and entrepreneurs put in longer hours. As a result, you can sometimes reach your prospect directly by calling during off hours. The best times to try this are early morning—7:00 A.M. to 9:00 A.M.; lunchtime—noon to 1:00 P.M.; or late afternoon/early evening—5:00 P.M. to 7:00 P.M.

Be aware of your prospect's reaction to being "caught" answering the phone at these hours. Some like it. They feel less pressured and more relaxed than during official business hours and may be more willing to talk. You can always develop a sense of camaraderie with a comment like "I see you're working late like me. We seem to do that a lot in our business, don't we?" But say this only if you can be sincere. Don't say it if you feel phony.

On the other hand, if you sense the prospect has been caught off-guard and is uncomfortable with the fact that you've reached him or her, quickly explain who you are and why you are calling, ask if it's a convenient time, and if it's not, make an appointment to call back at a specific time and date. What you'll find most often, though, is that the prospect's initial shock and reluctance quickly wear off, and most will happily chat with you for a few minutes.

The Answer/Ask Strategy

The Answer/Ask, or A/A, Strategy was invented by the sales trainer Bill Bishop and is described in his newsletter, *Master Prospector*. The technique basically involves "turning the tables" on secretaries, receptionists, and other filters by answering their questions *with a question.*

As Bill explains, "My A/A Strategy is a technique guaranteed to get you past the secretary to the decision maker. The First A stands for 'answer.' This means you answer filters' questions, instead of playing evasive cat-and-mouse games that tell filters you are a salesperson.

"The second A stands for 'ask,' meaning you ask a question in between your initial answer to their question, and before they ask you another filtering question.

"To summarize, 'A/A' means 'answer/ask.' Don't be evasive. Answer their initial filtering question, and before they can ask another, you ask them a question. This prevents them from asking additional filtering questions, and you'll get the decision maker on the line."

Continues Bill, "Taking the 'A/A' a step further, you can answer their question with a question." This is the way Bill's technique works. Let's look at an example.

RECEPTIONIST: Good morning. Acme Widgets.

BILL: Mr. Big, please.

RECEPTIONIST: May I tell him who's calling?

BILL: Would you tell him you have Bill Bishop holding, please?

See the technique? If you simply answer "It's Bill Bishop calling," you set the secretary up for her next screening question, designed to block your call. But instead, when you answer with a question—"Would you tell him you have Bill Bishop holding, please?"—the reasonable response is for the filter to answer in the affirmative and put you through. Naturally, the secretary or receptionist will say "Yes, I'll tell him." What else is she going to say? "No, I won't tell him?"

Once in a while you'll get a tough filter who will come back with the second filtering question. Here's how the A/A strategy handles it:

RECEPTIONIST: And who are you with, Mr. Bishop?

BILL: Would you tell him my company is Bill Bishop Associates, please?

Again, if you just said, "My company is Bill Bishop Associates," the likely response would be "And what is this in reference to?" or "Does he know you?" But when you say, "Would you tell him my company is Bill Bishop Associates, please?" the natural response is "Yes, I'll tell him." Can you imagine the receptionist saying "No, I won't tell him"?

Suppose you get that ultratough filter who bounces back with a third screening question. Here's an example:

> RECEPTIONIST: And what is this in reference to?
> BILL: Would you please tell him that I'm calling about [the purpose of your call]?

The beauty of "answer/ask" questions is they can't get a no answer from the filter. Consider how awkward a filter's responses would be:

> BILL: Would you please tell him I'm with Bill Bishop Associates?
> RECEPTIONIST: No.

Filters generally won't answer the question negatively. Instead, they signify a yes by connecting you to the prospect.

Will answer/ask eliminate all secretarial screening? No. But it will reduce the number of screening questions and get you through in a certain percentage of cases where you wouldn't normally have been connected.

CALLBACKS

Here's a frequent scenario:

> YOU: Mr. Prospect, please.
> SECRETARY: Mr. Prospect is in a meeting. Would you like to leave your name and number so I can ask him to call you back?

There are two ways to handle this. The first is to put the burden on the prospect's shoulders by leaving your name and number and saying "Yes, please have him call me." While this is convenient for you, there are some dangers in this, as Bill Bishop points out. Namely, here's what might happen:

1. You might not be in when the prospect calls back and many people don't like talking to answering services, answering machines, or voice-mail systems.
2. You'll be in, but on another call and will have to put the first prospect on hold while you take the second prospect's call.
3. The prospect, suspecting you're trying to sell something, probably won't return your call.
4. The prospect returns your call and you answer, "Good morning! John Doe Consulting Service!" The prospect's thoughts are confirmed that you called to *sell* and not to buy.
5. The prospect calls, isn't fazed by the way your phone is answered, and catches you by surprise. You've forgotten his name and why you called him. Imagine what he thinks!

"I must get two or three calls every day from stockbrokers who leave their name and a callback number for me," says Bishop. "The return call goes something as follows."

HIM: Hello, this is Bob Broker.
BILL BISHOP: This is Bill Bishop returning your call.
HIM: Uh, well, ahh, ugh, gee er, umm . . . Why did I call you, Bill?

"Well," continues Bishop, "if he doesn't know why he called, I'm sure not going to help him figure it out. The moral is, don't leave your name and number." Instead, advises Bishop, follow this script:

SECRETARY: Mr. Prospect is in a meeting. Would you like to leave your name and number so I can ask him to call you back?

YOU: I'd like to, but I'm going out shortly. When do you think he'll be free?

SECRETARY: Well, let's see, it's ten-twenty A.M., so I'd say he'd call you about ten forty-five A.M.

YOU: Gee, unfortunately I'll be gone by then. When do you think I should try him again?

SECRETARY: Well, he likes to come in real early—around seven-fifteen—so you could likely catch him then.

YOU: Okay, I'll try him later today or tomorrow morning, okay?

SECRETARY: Okay. Bye.

Notice how everything you say ends with a question (the "answer/ask" technique in action). You learn precisely when the prospect will be in to receive your call, all without being sneaky or evasive.

TREAT THEM RIGHT

Perhaps the best attitude to take with secretaries, receptionists, and other filters and gatekeepers is to treat them with respect and dignity, rather than view them as roadblocks to be pushed out of your way.

Many, many of your competitors treat secretaries with indifference or even as inferiors, never stopping to realize there's a human being behind that telephone headset or word processor. If you do acknowledge the secretaries' existence and treat them decently, with common courtesy, you'll be at the top of their list of favorite people.

And if you think this goodwill doesn't translate into action, you're wrong. A secretary who likes you will go out of his or her way to put your call through, make sure your fax gets on the boss's desk, and in general do everything to help you succeed. A secretary who dislikes you will sabotage your efforts, helping your competitors beat you out for the business.

You don't have to shower the assistants with gifts to win them over. Learning their names and calling them by name when you telephone is a nice first step; many people never bother to learn the names of secretaries or receptionists. If, after a few calls, they recognize you and seem inclined toward making a few pleasantries over the phone, do likewise. Getting to know and treating the secretary as a person is the best way you can get her or him on your side.

At our office, we enter the secretary's name as well as the prospect's name in our contact database record for that company. We gather the same kind of personal information—birthdays, hobbies, interests, children—on secretaries as we do on their bosses. We treat the secretary as a real person, not just a barrier between us and the decision maker. This makes him or her our ally, not our enemy.

WHAT ABOUT VOICE MAIL?

An assistant can be persuaded to help you, but a voice-mail system can't. More and more prospects, especially in corporations, use voice mail as a way of screening calls, including sales calls. This makes it tougher, but not impossible, to reach them.

One technique that works, as we already discussed, is calling them at off-hours. They won't be expecting calls early in the morning or late at night, and will often answer the phone themselves.

Another technique, one that can work only once for any given prospect, is to leave a "partial message," giving the prospect the impression that the rest of your message accidentally got cut off by the voice-mail system. You start talking a second before the voice-mail system beeps to allow you to record, so your message sounds something like this: " . . . so give me a call and we can discuss it. That's Joe Jones at 212-555-5555. I look forward to hearing from you."

The prospect has your contact information but thinks the first part was cut off, so has no clue as to why you called. Her curiosity is aroused, and besides, she doesn't want to risk not connecting with you if the call in fact is important to her.

This technique will get prospects to return your calls 20 to 40 percent of the time you leave a voice-mail message. But you can use it only once for each prospect. If you use it a second time, you immediately reveal that you have tricked the prospect with a sales technique, and you will probably lose her as a customer.

Another effective method is to leave a voice-mail message saying who you are, and that you will call the prospect tomorrow at such and such a time. When you call and you get a secretary, she will ask, "Is he expecting your call?" Because of the voice-mail message you left the day before, your answer is "Yes." This works beautifully when you get the secretary or receptionist on the call-back. If you get voice mail again, don't leave another message but keep trying until a human picks up the phone.

☎ _Ten_ ☎

Follow-up

Don't you hate it when you talk with a prospect who seems to have an urgent need for your products or services and this happens? You drop everything to do an estimate, you begin to clear your schedule to make room for this new project, you submit the quote, and then you wait. And you wait.

When you don't hear back, you call to follow up and the prospect says he hasn't had time to look at your proposal yet. You wait some more, and though you dread it, you call again. Or maybe you don't. In any case, you never hear from him again.

This happens all the time—not just to you—and there's little you can do about it. Here's what it may look like from your prospect's perspective:

On the day you spoke with the prospect, this project was at the top of his list. But the next day, something else came along that took priority and kept pushing the project further and further away, until it was on a permanent back burner. He never bothered to let you know, probably because he didn't have time. Or, more likely, he got caught up in his own world.

The reality is you can't control your prospects, and it's almost impossible to know in advance whether a lead is a good one or whether the project you're quoting will go anywhere. On first impression, you can't usually tell the literature collectors from the bona fide prospects. Sometimes you may want to say, "Tell me either yes or no, but don't keep me hanging on like this." But they can't. Only time will tell.

What you can control is how you spend your time. And you decide how vigorously you want to pursue each project and how much time you can afford to devote to each prospect. In order to do that, you have to rate your prospects and prioritize your efforts toward them.

Fast Response Prevents Lost Sales

To satisfy anyone's urgent need, have the basic information about your business ready and faxable (three pages maximum). Then, if necessary, take your time to put together a more tailored package and mail it.

When you promise to send information, be sure to send it promptly. Sloppy lead handling looks really bad, and, as the marketing consultant David Wood writes, "Failure to fulfill your first commitment to a client establishes you as unreliable and undependable. In addition, the sooner it gets there, the fresher your conversation is in his or her mind and the more quickly it can be continued."

Follow-up Strategies That Work

These days, people rarely return phone calls. This omission is unprofessional but it's a reality. So now more than ever it's up to you to follow up.

For qualified leads (i.e., hot prospects and especially those who have contacted you) follow-up calls are a must. The call should be made approximately a week after the information is sent out, on any day but Monday.

For cold prospects (people who don't know you), follow-up calls can only help. It's unrealistic to think that you could do follow-up calls to everyone on your calling list, but you could certainly make calls to the top 10 percent of potential customers on the list.

Chances are they got your mail and it's in a pile somewhere. Your phone call will resurrect your piece of paper from that pile, and because timing is everything in marketing, that follow-up call could provide the final push needed to get the project on track. They might surprise you with "You know, I've been meaning to call you."

From the time you make your first contact with the prospect until the time they are ready to buy from you, these follow-up activities are all effective:

Make a follow-up phone call.

Send an e-mail.

Fax a note.

Send a birthday or holiday card.

Send articles of interest.

Send any publicity you get.

Jot down any ideas relating to their project.

When making follow-up contacts, these phrases can help warm up the prospect and set the right tone:

Thanks for speaking to me.

I know your time is valuable.

As we discussed . . .

I look forward to continuing our conversation.

Call me with any questions.

Call me to continue the conversation.

Let me know if I can be of any help.

The following phrases may also be helpful:

We haven't spoken in a while and I wanted to check in and see if anything has changed.

Perhaps you are in a better position than when we first spoke to use our services.

I was wondering if you are still planning to buy this type of product?

Some additional tips and thoughts about follow-up:

- Follow-up is marketing to the same group over and over.
- Don't forget to follow up with your former clients.
- Make follow-up letters brief. Use a Post-it. It's just a reminder, to jog their memory.
- Always call to make sure your information was received.

UNDERSTANDING PROSPECT RESPONSE

Many telesellers read too much into prospects' responses, worry unduly, or spend too much time trying to decipher what the prospects really mean, when most of the time, what they mean is pretty much what they said. The following guidelines may be helpful in dealing with prospects in sales situations:

What they say: "I have a project. Could you send your information?"

What you hear: They want me.

What they mean: They're gathering information on potential candidates.

What to do: Send or fax your info. Follow up in a week.

What they say: "Your info is here somewhere but I haven't looked at it yet."

What you hear: They chose someone else.

What they mean: Other things have come up and the project isn't as urgent.

What to do: Ask when to call back and keep in touch.

What they say: "I've looked over your materials and they look interesting, but we haven't decided what direction to take. We'll be in touch."

What you hear: They chose someone else.

What they mean: Things have changed and the project isn't as important anymore.

What to do: Keep in touch quarterly for other possible projects.

What they say: Nothing. No callback.

What you hear: They chose someone else.

What they mean: They're busy with other things or maybe they did choose someone else. It's not the end of the world.

What to do: Keep in touch every few months by fax, mail, and phone.

WHICH PROSPECTS SHOULD BE FOLLOWED UP?

You can't follow up with everyone and the good news is, you don't have to. But in order to decide whom to pursue and whom to let go, you have to determine their value to you—qualify them, in marketing lingo.

The big question is: Is there a fit? Don't be so eager to get a project that you fail to consider a prospect's fitness for you. Here is a list of questions to ask yourself about each prospect that will help you decide whether they are a good fit for you:

BUSINESS POTENTIAL

1. Why aren't they still working with their previous vendor?
2. Do they have future needs? Immediate needs?
3. Is there potential for ongoing business?

THE DECISION-MAKING PROCESS

1. Is your contact the decision maker?
2. Are there several layers of bureaucracy to deal with?

(cont'd)

---

3. Can they afford you?
4. Can they pay a percentage up front?

PERSONALITY/WORKING STYLE

1. Does your contact respect your time and labor?
2. Do they require a lot of hand holding?
3. Do they understand that you have other clients?
4. Do they buy on the basis of price? Quality? Both?
5. Do they respect your professional boundaries?
6. Do they do business honestly and with integrity?
7. Do you feel comfortable with them?

YOUR FITNESS FOR THEM

1. Does this project fit into your specialty?
2. Could you refer someone who would be a better fit?
3. Do they require more time, service, or technical expertise than you have available?

Once you have given each prospect a rating, determine your strategy. Here's a sample rating system and strategy:

HOT—Has an immediate need. Follow up right away.

WARM—Will have a need soon. Ask how they want you to follow up.

COOL—May have future needs. Keep on the mailing list and contact quarterly.

COLD—Worth one call to see that they received information. Otherwise, let them come to you.

The key point: Not every prospect should be followed up on. And not all prospects should be given an equal follow-up effort. Spend the most time and effort following up with your hot prospects. Give others only occasional reminders of your existence.

MEASURING RESULTS

"I don't like to assess success simply by measuring response," says Ilise Benun, publisher of *The Art of Self-Promotion* quarterly newsletter. "There are too many unknowns that figure into the ultimate results. This is a lesson I've learned many times, but I'll never forget one time several years ago.

"I spoke at a conference that was very poorly publicized and, thus, poorly attended. My workshop had five people. I spontaneously changed the format of my presentation, put us into an intimate circle, and gave a highly interactive self-promotion workshop (which I wouldn't have been able to do with a big group). It turned out to be extremely productive and everyone left feeling great, myself included. If asked the next day how many people showed up, the number five would have drawn a groan from anyone. But more is not always better and it wasn't that day. A year later; one of those five became an important client for me."

Of course response is important. But while response is indeed significant, it's not all there is. I know it's difficult to imagine that those who receive phone calls but don't respond are affected in a positive way. But don't assume they're not.

There are too many unknowns; people's needs and interests are constantly changing. For example, you'll never know how many people put your brochure in that infamous "in" basket, which they really do plan to go through just as soon as they get a free minute. You'll never know how many people file your material for future use.

You'll never know how many people pass your catalogue along to a colleague who may be calling soon. You'll never know how many people are presenting an idea to their boss with the intention to work with you but haven't yet received approval.

Yes, they're intangible and unquantifiable but all of these effects can have an impact on the results of your promotional efforts and you'll never be able to trace them back to any one promotion.

But you have to measure something. You need some way to know if what you're doing is working, a gauge by which to judge. If you need some hard facts, go ahead and measure response. Make five hundred cold calls. Count how many people respond positively, and keep track of how many jobs result from that one phone effort. Just keep in mind that it's not the whole picture.

Give each marketing effort six months, minimum. More often than not, it's not just one communication that brings a client; it's the succession of messages. It can take four to nine calls to make a sale.

When you do make a judgment, take a wide view and go with your gut. You will know if what you're doing is worth the time and energy involved. You will know if you enjoy the process. You will know if people like it, remember it, notice it. You will know if, over the course of a year of consistent marketing, your business has grown.

You will know if it works. It will show at your bottom line.

TIMING

How often should you follow up? There's no set formula, only some guidelines.

A good starting point is the "Rule of Seven," formulated by the marketing expert Dr. Jeffrey Lant. It states that to penetrate the buyer's consciousness and make significant penetration in a given market, you have to contact those people a minimum of seven times within an 18-month period. This is slightly more than once every quarter. Although your frequency may be less or more, seven contacts within 18 months, or four to five contacts within a year, is a good starting point for a follow-up plan.

You can modify this plan to suit your preferences. It's really up to you. Do what works. Don't get locked into a formula. If you get better results contacting warm prospects monthly, do so . . . as long as you keep below a frequency they will find annoying or offensive.

How do you know if you are following up too frequently? If one or two prospects complain or seem annoyed, modify your schedule to accommodate just them. But if 5 percent or more respond negatively to your frequency of follow-up, scale back on follow-up for that entire group of prospects. Use prospects' feedback to guide you in your efforts.

What are the best times of day and days of the week to make follow-up calls? Opinions differ. For business prospects, Tuesday, Wednesday, and Thursday are the best follow-up days. Mondays people are too cranky, and Fridays they are too eager to get to the weekend. Mornings are usually better than the afternoons, because most people have more energy.

Follow-up Scripts for Typical Situations

When you follow up, you will often encounter prospects with an attitude. That attitude may be positive and friendly. But more often, it is reserved, guarded, or adversarial. Here are some ideas for handling these different situations.

You Call and Find the Prospect Friendly or Receptive.

Here's a rare thrill: You call and the prospect actually seems happy to hear from you again! Don't get excited or interpret levels of commitment and enthusiasm that may not be there. Some people are naturally effervescent and outgoing, yet may not have the slightest interest in dealing with you. Others who are stony and silent may surprise you with an order.

When the prospects are friendly or receptive, match their enthusiasm, but don't exceed it. Prospects resent it when salespeople misinterpret friendliness as interest or commitment. They resent being pushed to a place they are not ready to go. Mirror the prospects' level of energy, but let their responses guide you. Don't push to close a sale or an appointment until you get signals they're ready to do so.

If you are not certain whether the prospect is ready to take action, during a lull in the conversation or toward the end, ask, "What's the next step?" or "What do you want to happen next?" If the prospects want to buy, they'll tell you what they need next from you to make a buying decision. Provide it.

Certainly you should always seek to get to the next step in the buying prospect. Push the prospect, but do it gently. Don't rush prospects, because it doesn't work, and often backfires.

Many salespeople try to achieve a different next step than the prospect asked for. It's okay to try to do what you want as well as what they want. But don't ignore or refuse prospect requests. One sales training institution teaches its students, "Never send literature, even if the prospect asks for it." This is ridiculous. Can you imagine calling up a company, asking for a brochure, and being told, "No, we can't send one." Can you imagine your prospects' reaction if you said this to them? It's absurd.

You Call and Find the Prospect Neutral or Reserved.

More often, the prospect will be slightly cool to you when you call to follow up. This doesn't mean she is not interested. But obviously, if she were ready to buy at that second, she probably would have called you instead of the other way around. You are interrupting her activity of the moment to try and sell her something. So why be surprised if you receive a reception that's lukewarm at best?

You can do several things to warm up the call. Of course, ask, "Am I catching you at a bad time?" If the prospect seems busy or says she is busy, say, "I understand how busy you are. Do you have three minutes now?" When you tell prospects the entire call will take less than three minutes, they become more comfortable, because they realize you aren't going to try to keep them tied up.

A short conversational exchange on a slightly personal note can help here too. Comment on the weather, or the World Series, or some other fairly neutral topic. If the prospect makes such a comment, pick up the thread and go with it for half a minute or so.

With contact-management software (discussed later in this chapter), you gain the advantage of having all data about the prospect in front of you on a computer screen as you talk. If the prospect mentioned she was going to Hawaii last time you talked, ask her how it was. If he was playing in a golf tournament, ask him how it went. You get the idea.

How long you continue the call depends on whether the prospect warms up. If she gets into a chatty mood, keep the conversation going while steering it toward your objective. If she remains distant or cool, or seems pressed for time, respect that and keep the call brief. Use your own judgment here.

You Call and Find the Prospect Negative or Unreceptive.

"Am I catching you at a bad time?" works well here too. It either gets him to drop the stuffed-shirt act and behave in a friendlier fashion, or prompts him to share with you that he is busy, in which case you set a time for a callback.

Do not assume there is something wrong if the prospect seems distant or cold. He may be busy, under pressure, working against a deadline. Maybe his wife is divorcing him, his sales are lousy, his child is ill, or he has lost his biggest customer. A poor reception doesn't mean there is an objection to you or your call. It just means now is not a good time. If that's the case, the best move is to find out a good time . . . and call back then.

You Call and Get Blocked by the Secretary or Receptionist.

The last two times you called you reached the prospect, no problem. But now you can't reach her. Instead, you always get the secretary. Or the receptionist.

Again, this doesn't mean the prospect is deliberately ducking your calls—although if she is busy or not ready to buy, that may be the case. It usually means she has someone else picking up the phone because she is too busy to talk to anyone—she's not singling you out for special treatment because you're a salesperson.

Chapter 9 gives dialogues for getting past the secretary. One of the most common screening questions is "Is he expecting your call?" If the callback is scheduled, the answer, "Yes, we had an appointment to talk today at this time," is easy and will often get past the secretarial blockade.

We have an even better technique at my office: We include each secretary's name in our sales database. And we consider them as a first contact rather than a barrier to be overcome. Therefore, instead of trying to fool the secretaries or bully our way past them, we talk to them as people and make them our allies in reaching the boss. Some even like us so much, they do some of the selling for us, urging the boss to buy from us instead of the other suppliers who treat secretaries like second-class citizens.

You Call and Are Told, "We're Looking at Other Suppliers."

The critical issue is not whether they are interviewing other people, but whether they have made a decision to choose someone else and have made a commitment to do business with that supplier.

If they have, you're probably sunk—for now. But keep in touch. The vendor they've chosen may not work out. Or the prospects may have additional needs. Use follow-ups to remind them you are available.

When a prospect chooses someone else, don't sulk. The decision is already made. If you say they made a bad choice—even if you believe it—they'll get angry. No one likes hearing that.

People want to believe they made the right choice. So when your prospects choose a competitor, congratulate them. Say they made a good choice and should be happy. This creates a favorable impression. Then gently remind them you're available if additional needs arise. This leaves the door open to future business. Never criticize or degrade the prospect's decision. Why burn bridges?

If the prospect hasn't made a decision yet, say: "Will you do me a favor? Before you make your final selection, call me, and let's talk briefly . . . whether we're the firm you select or not." The purpose? To give you a chance to talk with the prospect one last time before the decision is made. If you reach the prospect before he or she has committed to someone else, there's still a chance of getting the business. On the other hand, if the next time you talk with the prospect, the choice has already been made, there's little to zero chance of changing the prospect's mind—at least for the time being.

You Call and Are Told, "We've Looked It Over and We're Not Interested."

Again, this isn't necessarily a rejection of you. It's possible the product doesn't meet their needs, or the need has changed or vanished.

Still, you want to find out more. Maybe another one of your products would meet the requirement, but your prospect doesn't even know you sell it. Or maybe your service still fits his new need, but you have to help him see it.

How do you find out the reason why he's not interested? One way is to be direct: "When we last spoke, you seemed very interested. I'm curious. What happened?"

Another way is to act as if the selling part of the conversation is over—since he told you he's not buying—and get him to confide in you. Say, "I understand I'm not going to sell you anything today. And I'm going to take your name out of our prospect database so we don't bother you anymore. But now that it's over, let me ask, what did we do wrong? What could we have done differently to get you to say yes?" Often the prospect will reveal the real objection, which, once in the open, can sometimes be overcome.

Strategies for Getting Unanswered Calls Returned

As we noted earlier, there is an unfortunate tendency in business today not to return calls. What can you do?

One method is to send a short fax. It tells the prospect, "I've been trying to reach you without success. Please indicate your preference below." Then have a series of check-off boxes the prospect can check and fax back to you that read something like this:

[ ] *I've just been very busy. Try me on (date)_____.*

[ ] *Now is not the right time. Try me on (date)_____.*

[ ] *I'm no longer interested because (please give reason)_____.*

Many prospects will respond. If they check one of the first two boxes, call back on the date specified. If they check the last box, and the reason they are no longer interested is an objection you can overcome, call or fax a reply.

KEEPING TRACK OF PROSPECTS (WHEN THEY'RE NOT READY)

If none of your prospects fell between the cracks, isn't it just possible that you'd have enough business? Fewer people would be so frantic about getting new business if they were on top of all the leads that came their way, responded promptly to requests for information, and followed them all the way through.

Call it apathy or just plain disorganization (it sometimes looks to me like sabotage), but without proper management, leads and referrals do fall between the cracks and, alas, much business is lost.

Often it's the details that prevent you from following up. To do it properly, you must have everything in one place: phone numbers, notes from previous conversations, price quotes. You can use a manual system, such as a tickler file, but that will only work if you remember to open the file cabinet. Other manual systems include appointment books, wall schedulers, calendars, three-ring notebooks, hanging files organized by month and day, and index cards in recipe file boxes.

In theory, these systems are simple. You note all relevant information about each prospect on a separate index card or sheet of paper. Cards and sheets are arranged not alphabetically, but according to when the next follow-up call is to take place.

This works. But there are drawbacks. As the number of prospects and customers in your sales database grows, paper systems become cumbersome: there are too many cards, too many sheets, too many files to deal with. Also, the paper files can only be retrieved according to the way they are organized, which is by callback date. If you want to look up information on a prospect, you won't be able to find the file unless you are lucky enough to remember the callback date.

The computer solves these problems. Put your sales database on your computer. You can use software to schedule follow-up calls. But at the same time, you can instantly retrieve any file by customer name, company name, state, or whatever other criteria you choose. So prospect files don't get lost, and vital information is always just a click of the mouse away.

Nowadays there are loads of software packages to help you do what they call contact management. My intention here is not to review software programs but merely to tell you how easy Act! and Telemagic for Windows can make following up. I can't compare them to other packages since they are the only ones we've ever used in my office, except for LeasePower 5, which I discuss below.

But I can tell you that when we turn on the computer in the morning (because I've already scheduled the tasks), it is all right there and all we have to do is make the calls. Nothing falls between the cracks. The program tells us whom we have to call that day, what we discussed last time, the date we last spoke with them, the topic of today's conversation—even what time to call them! It all comes up on your screen automatically. So you don't miss follow-ups you promised to make.

Another good contact-management program is LeasePower 5, but this is designed specifically for and available only to resellers. If you are a reseller and want more information, contact Studebaker-Worthington Leasing Corp., 800-645-7242.

You don't have to buy contact-management software to track prospects and sales on your computer. You can buy a database program and design your own custom system. But with so many good contact managers on the market at prices ranging from $95 to $1,500, I'd recommend investing in one and learning how to use it. The advantage: It's already customized to track prospects and leads.

Whether you are shopping for a contact manager (they are sometimes called "sales database programs" or "personal information managers") or planning to design your own, the software should be able to capture the following information on each prospect:

Name

Title

Company

Business phone number

Home phone

E-mail address

Web site address

Fax number

Address

City

State

Zip code

Country

Source of inquiry (how did they find out about you?)

Date of inquiry

Description of their product or service requirements

A record of follow-ups—dates and discussion summaries

The date for the next follow-up call.

The software should have the following capabilities:

Retrieve any prospect file by company name

Retrieve any prospect file by prospect name

Automatically schedule follow-up calls

Keep track of prospect contacts

Print a complete list of prospects with company names, addresses, phone numbers

Sort and print prospect lists by alphabetical order, city, state, zip code, or other criteria you specify.

Additional capabilities that are nice to have but are not indispensable include:

Form letters and custom sales letters

Generation of quotes and proposals

Product database (items you sell and their prices)

On-line product literature or fact sheets

Mail-merge for sending out direct mailings

Automatic dial-up of prospects' phone numbers

Compatibility with other applications.

WHAT IF THEY *STILL* WON'T CALL YOU BACK?

There may be times when you call prospects repeatedly and don't get through, despite the fact that they asked you to call, requested information, or were referred by a business associate. Let's say you've called numerous times and a prospect so far has not returned your call. Should you call again?

That's really up to you and how far you want to pursue the lead. Some salespeople might say, "Persist until you get through." I think there's probably a limit after which you give up—perhaps two, three, or four callbacks, but certainly no more.

Here's a strategy you can use with the secretary on the final call.

SECRETARY: Joe Smith's office.

YOU: This is [your name] calling again. Is he in?

SECRETARY: He's not in. Would you care to leave a message?

YOU: Yes, but . . . Excuse me, what is your name?

SECRETARY: Mary.

YOU: Well, Mary, maybe you can help me. Joe requested information on our Danglemaster Two Thousand Processor, and I've called four times and left four messages, but he hasn't returned my calls. If he's interested in my service then I still want to help him and will keep trying, but if he's not interested, I don't want to keep bothering you or waste your time. Could you do me a favor and ask him if he's still interested in the service and if so, when would be a good time to talk about his particular needs?

SECRETARY: Yes, I can do that.

YOU: Thanks, Mary, I appreciate it. Today is Monday. Would it be okay if you could ask him today or tomorrow, and I'll call you back on Wednesday to find out where we stand?

SECRETARY: That would be okay.

YOU: Okay, Mary, I'll call you Wednesday. And thanks.

If you still get the same old brush-off Wednesday, forget about the lead.

But more likely, Mary will give you the information you asked for—either a time to call Joe and discuss his needs or the information that she relayed the message and that yes, Joe got your material, but he'll call you if he needs you, and don't call him.

If that's the case, you might ask Mary whether you can at least put Joe on your mailing list. When she says yes—and she probably will—you can follow up in the future by mail a couple of times.

☎ *Eleven* ☎

Closing the Sale

C "Closing" means getting the order. For product sellers, this means getting a signed contract or purchase order. For service sellers, it means getting a prospect to agree to retain you, or at least to make a tentative commitment contingent upon final approval of your fee and contract.

Many businesspeople understandably don't enjoy pressuring prospects and would prefer that potential clients close themselves by saying, "Okay, let's go, I'm ready to buy." Others, many of whom work on Wall Street, enjoy closing and pushing for the order.

Unfortunately, fewer and fewer prospects close themselves these days. Consumers are more hesitant to spend money and more likely to examine each purchasing decision more carefully than they did ten years ago. As a result, you are going to have to bring up and negotiate the final details of the deal if you want to get the order.

Closing requires that you come right out and say to the prospect, "I would like to have you as a customer. May we get started?" This makes many professionals uncomfortable. Many of us were taught that asking for the order is inappropriate. It is not.

"What Do You Want to Happen Next?"

Ilise Benun has developed a wonderful line that can be used both during the intermediate stages of the sales cycle as well as at closing. It's effective in moving the prospect one step closer to a final decision in a way that is not adversarial and does not make you seem desperate or overeager for the order.

When you reach a point where it seems you should move forward, but the prospect doesn't seem to know what to do next and doesn't suggest a course of action, say to the prospect, "What do you want to happen next?" or "What's the next step?" This prompts the prospect to come right out and tell you exactly what is required to consummate the transaction.

You probably get nervous about closing because you don't want to appear too pushy, and you're also afraid the prospect will say "No" or "I'm not ready yet"—both of which do happen.

On the other hand, if you want to make the sale, it is up to you to initiate the next and final step—the close. The prospect doesn't know exactly how to proceed and is looking to you for guidance.

"What do you want to happen next?" signals that further action should be taken and also says, subtly, "It's time to buy." But it gives the prospect the option of proceeding at a pace he is comfortable with. Also, it's nonadversarial: You are not telling the prospect what to do. You are asking him what he wants done.

"What do you want to happen next?" works. Try it!

You Might Hate Closing, but You Have to Do It Anyway . . .

Closing is necessary because it overcomes prospect resistance, inertia, and ignorance.

Prospects are *resistant* because, like most people, they hate to part with money. They suffer from *inertia*, the natural tendency of all objects, animate and inanimate, to resist action and movement. Worse, they are also, to a degree, *ignorant*, in that even if they want to buy from you, they're not quite sure what to order, how much to order, or how to go about it. Do they sign a contract? Write you a letter? Phone? Pay some money up front? Try your system for 30 days? Lease, rent, or buy your equipment?

When people are unsure what to do next, their choice is to do *nothing*. By closing, you provide prospects with welcome guidance on what the next step is and how to take it.

So if you want the prospect's business, you've got to step forward and ask for it.

Closing Techniques You Can Use

Get Prospects to Invest Time and Effort in Your Relationship.

The more time and effort prospects invest in making the decision whether to buy from you, the more likely you are to close the sale.

This doesn't mean you should waste prospects' time or make it deliberately difficult for them to communicate with you. Far from it.

But it does mean that if you can get prospects to invest their time and effort in a relationship with you before you are officially retained to provide product or perform services on a paid basis, you are more likely to get the order than someone with whom prospects have not invested a lot of time and effort.

"If a client asks you to sit in on a developmental meeting, whether you are paid for that effort are not, you are the vendor of choice," says the business writer Paul D. Davis. "I have never, except once, had a client give an assignment to someone else after I helped with the concept and planning of that project."

Consider this scenario. You have been talking with a prospect on and off for the past six months. You've exchanged lots of calls, letters, and information. Now she's ready to hire a consultant to handle her firm's outplacement. Whom will she be more likely to hire—you, a person with whom she is already familiar and comfortable, or your competitor, who called her for the first time last week? Unless your competitor offers some tremendous advantage or proprietary method you don't have, you stand the better chance of getting the business.

For this reason, it pays to get prospects involved with you at an early stage, even before money is exchanged or contracts are signed.

Think about how you can involve your prospects early. Do you survey their employees? Give them a demonstration? Get them to attend your free seminar? Have them watch a videotape? Install a system in their office for a free 30-day trial? The more time prospects invest, the more eager they will be to move the relationship forward on a productive (and for you, a paid) basis.

Incremental Closes.

In sales lingo, closes are categorized as "major" or "minor." A *major close* is when a prospect says, "Yes, we'll take it." Before that occurs, there will typically be a series of minor, or incremental, closes. An *incremental close* involves getting a prospect to agree to different ideas, concepts, and suggestions you propose as you talk your way to the close of the sale.

Basically, this technique involves getting prospects to say yes to a number of miniproposals you present orally. Each miniproposal covers one of the items or conditions of the sale. Taken together, they are the total package you want to sell the prospect.

After getting prospects to say yes to each miniproposal, you then sum up the total package, noting that they have agreed to each point. Finally, you restate your proposition in its entirety and get prospects to finalize the agreement.

Here's how I used this technique recently with a prospect who wanted me to write a direct-mail piece to generate sales leads for his firm:

ME: So, Mr. Jones, I understand you are looking for a direct-mail piece to generate sales leads that will result in new clients for your company.

PROSPECT: Yes.

ME: As we've discussed, the best format would be a sales letter with a brochure and reply card.

PROSPECT: Yes

ME: And you would prefer that it be mailed in a personally addressed, standard-size business envelope—

PROSPECT: Yes, that's correct.

ME: We've gone over my fee schedule and you understand that it's $1,500 to write the brochure, $950 for a one-page letter, and $150 for the reply card?

PROSPECT: Fine. I have no problem with that.

ME: And you would like to have a first draft of the copy in two weeks or sooner, is that right?

PROSPECT: Yes.

ME: And you'll handle all the graphics and design of the piece yourself using your Macintosh system and Page-Maker.

PROSPECT: Yes.

ME: Okay. So let me prepare an agreement that spells out

Closing the Sale

that I'll be writing for you a lead-generating direct-mail package, with letter, brochure, and reply card, for a fee of $2,600 total, and it's due two weeks from today.
PROSPECT: Fine.

See the technique? First I get prospects to agree to each point concerning the deal we are making. Once they've done that, how can they say no to my final proposition, as it merely sums up a number of points they've already said yes to?

A series of small or incremental closes in which you get prospects to say yes step by step to the deal as you've structured it makes it easy to go for the final close, where it is almost impossible for prospects to refuse you.

Of course, if prospects say no to one of your intermediate closes, then it becomes an objection, and you either must overcome that objection or remove that particular element from the agreement you are trying to finalize.

Act As If You Already Have the Business.

This doesn't mean you pour the foundation, write the report, conduct the seminar, do the survey, ship the merchandise, install the equipment, or start the work. That would be premature and foolish.

When I say "Act as if you already have the order," I mean your tone, mannerisms, and words should exude confidence. Without being obvious or high-handed, you should behave as if your getting the order is a foregone conclusion, with fee negotiations, contracts, and purchase orders a mere formality standing in the way of your getting started. You want to get out of the "audition" mode and into a working relationship mode as soon as possible.

Successful telesellers are confident and decisive. They feel sure enough about their abilities to say to prospects, "We are best qualified. Our product can solve your problem and do it well. What are you waiting for? Sign on the dotted line and we'll get started."

Prospects want to hire people who appear to know what they're doing. This means being a man or woman of action. It's time for prospects to move forward, but inertia, laziness, or uncertainty prevents them from doing so. They look to you for guidance. You must take prospects by the hand and gently but forcefully get them to commit to action.

False modesty (or maybe genuine lack of confidence) prevents many of us from acting confidently. Unfortunately, this attitude only feeds prospects' natural inertia. It will not get you the sale you want, which means prospects will not benefit from the goods and services you provide.

When you act as if you already have the job, project, or order, the confident attitude will subtly alter the texture of the conversation between you and prospects. Instead of being in a *selling* mode, you'll be in a *working partnership* mode. Your comments will be directed toward understanding clients' requirements or helping to find the best solution for their problems, not desperately thinking of what you can say to persuade them to give you a retainer check or sign a contract.

Avoid Time-limited, High-pressure, Face-to-face Closing

In direct mail, having a time-limited offer is an extremely effective technique. Phrases like "Offer expires December 15," "Supplies are limited, order today!" and "This is a limited offer, and once it expires, it may never be repeated again" give prospects a genuine reason to respond now instead of later, which dramatically increases response rates.

But while most people are understanding and responsive to such time-limited offers in direct-mail situations, they resent such pressure in a selling situation.

Here are a few of my don'ts concerning pressure selling:

- *Don't* tell prospects, "I can give you this price, but only if you commit today." This makes you look sleazy and makes prospects extremely uncomfortable.
- *Don't* lie or say things that prospects will not believe. If business is scarce, and you're desperate to make the sale, don't try to pressure prospects by saying, "We're very busy and we only have one slot open on our schedule, so you need to sign up this week or we won't be able to take you on." Prospects will know you are lying.
- *Don't* use two-tier pricing, a low price if prospects buy today versus a higher price if prospects want to think about it and get back to you. As I've said, while this works effectively in direct-mail selling, it can backfire in tele-selling. Be careful.

Remove the Risk.

The fastest route to overcoming buyer resistance when attempting to close a sale is take the burden of risk off prospects' shoulders and place it on the shoulders of you, the seller.

One publisher selling monthly business newsletters removes all risk to purchase with this unconditional money-back guarantee: At any time during your subscription, if you feel the newsletter is not worth the money, you notify them and they will refund your entire subscription fee in full, without your having to return any of the issues. On a one-year subscription, they will do this even after you have received your twelfth issue, which is the last one in your subscription. That's how confident they are that their product is of value.

According to *Business Breakthroughs*, a newsletter for entrepreneurs, Jeff Lazerson, president of Portfolio Mortgage Corporation in Lake Forest, Illinois, offered prospects a $50 gift certificate to their favorite restaurant if they weren't satisfied with his service.

Two people cashed in on the guarantee offer. One was just taking advantage of him. The other, Lazerson admits in the article, was for a file that was botched. The total cost of the two gift certificates: $100. But the program brought in additional revenue to Portfolio Mortgage of a quarter million dollars.

Shifting the risk from buyer to seller won't sell people a product they don't want in the first place, nor will it be a solution to a problem they don't have (or do have but don't care about). It will, however, get many potential buyers—people who are interested but hesitate because of the cost, not knowing your firm, or another factor—to go ahead and place the order. It's very powerful to say to a prospect who is not sure, "Well, why don't you try it and if you don't like it, send it back and pay us nothing?"

Act Fast.

When prospects indicate they are ready to buy, act fast. Immediately write up a quotation, prepare the contract, or send an agreement. Have it in the prospect's hands within 48 hours. You can send it by first-class mail, Federal Express, or, if it's just a page or two, via fax or e-mail.

Why is prompt response important? Two reasons. First, it makes sense to get prospects to commit right away. If they have too much time to think about it, they may find additional reasons for delaying or deferring. The delay may also give your competitor time to move in.

Second, prospects judge you on first impressions and form their opinion of you largely on the basis of how you perform in the initial phases of any engagement or relationship. If you're tardy or indifferent about preparing the quotation or contract or about getting started on the assignment, it gives prospects cause to think you'll be even less motivated and caring later on. And that's not what they want.

CONSTANTLY CLOSING

When, exactly, can you consider the sale "closed"? When prospects call and say they're tentatively interested? When clients say, "Yes, go ahead"? When the contract is signed? When you get your check? When you drop your shipment off on the customer's loading dock and drive away in your truck?

In one sense the sale is never truly closed. You are constantly closing—that is, you're always striving to make sure customers are satisfied and pleased with you. You can't really consider the sale closed when you get the signed contract or purchase order, because clients can always cancel, and it may be difficult to collect all or even a portion of your fee if that happens.

One teleseller confided in me, "I consider the sale made when the buyer's check clears in my bank account." But even that isn't the end of it. You've got to perform as promised, or the customer might demand return of payment on the basis of nonperformance.

For many businesses the one-shot customer is the least profitable. The real money is made with repeat buyers and clients who retain you on a periodic or, even better, ongoing basis. The repeat business is where the biggest profits are. To get these repeat orders, your performance on the initial job must be superior.

Almost everything you do or say in the course of your relationship with the client determines whether you close that next sale. You are constantly closing this sale and the next. Selling does not end with the signed contract or purchase order but is ongoing throughout the life of the vendor-client relationship.

LET PROSPECTS HELP YOU CLOSE

Listen to your prospects. Frequently they will tell you word for word what they want to hear from you—indeed, what they *need* to hear from you—before they will buy from you. A technique that works well is to ask prospects what they want, then repeat it back to them in your own words. When prospects hear their requirements spoken by you, they will be confident that you truly understand what they need.

You must sell to prospects in the way they are comfortable buying, not the way you are comfortable selling. And this goes especially for the closing, which is the situation in which the prospect, faced with finally having to make a real decision, has the greatest level of fear and anxiety.

We have all been in situations where we haven't bought a product or service because the salesperson made us uncomfortable. To increase your chances of closing the sale, be in sync with the mood and personality of your prospects, and adjust your presentation accordingly.

For instance, tellesellers speak at an average rate of 150 words per minute or so. But they will speed up when calling New York City and slow down when calling Tennessee or Georgia, because they sell more effectively when the pace of their speech matches that of the person they're calling.

In the same way, training seminars on selling overseas advise international businesspeople to follow the local business customs of the client's country. After all, most people would rather buy from people who are like them rather than from people who are strange and different.

Now this doesn't mean you should be a chameleon, totally changing your stripes and colors to match whatever personality you think would be ideal for selling a particular prospect. This would be phony, and people can spot a phony.

However, it does pay to be sensitive to the prospect's personality and mood and to adjust your style within reason to match.

If prospects seem pressed for time, compress your sales pitch to accommodate their busy schedule and get to the close quickly. Be businesslike and don't waste time with idle chatter. Adjusting your presentation and style to the prospect's mood and personality, especially during the sensitive closing period, will improve your sales results and client relationships.

Become Comfortable with Closing

You may hate closing now. But most tellsellers I talk to tell me that over time they become more at ease with selling, more comfortable with the idea of asking for the order.

Here are a few suggestions for putting yourself more at ease with the concept of closing:

1. Remember, the worst the prospect can do is say no. And that's really not so terrible. There are plenty of other prospects out there for you. There's always tomorrow.
2. The situation need not be awkward or unpleasant if you maintain professional, cool, detached behavior at all times. If the prospect says no, it doesn't mean loss of dignity or face for you. Your inner mental attitude should be: "I'd like to help you, Mr. Prospect, but if you refuse to see the wisdom of buying from us, the loss is primarily yours, not mine."
3. Most sellers take the position that any customers who buy from them are doing them a favor. They aren't. Think of the transaction as an equal exchange of goods and services for money. Realize that your customers need you as much as you need them.
4. Embarrassment in asking for the order is natural but not logical. Obviously, the prospect knows you are trying to sell something. To sell something, you must ask for the order, and the prospect must give you the order. Therefore, the prospect *expects* you to ask for the order. If you delay it too long, the relationship may lose momentum and the sale may get off track or fizzle totally.

5. Avoid asking questions that can be answered with "yes" or "no." Part of your discomfort in closing comes from the fear and embarrassment of being too aggressive and being rejected. Rejection comes when the prospect says no. Prospects say no when they are made uncomfortable or are unduly pressured. Therefore you can avoid pressuring people and risking rejection by never asking a question that could be answered with "no."

For instance, if you feel ready to close, don't ask the prospect, "Would you like us to ship you a gross?" Instead, ask, "When would you want us to ship this—this week or early next month?" People's natural tendency when they are uncertain is to say no. But when you offer them a choice, their tendency is to select one of the options you've proposed.

Twelve

Customer Service:
Improving Teleselling Results

The greatest profits are generated not from initial sales but through repeat business and reorders.

Skillful selling can get a customer to buy from you once, maybe even twice. But unless customers are satisfied, they will not continue to favor you with their business.

Satisfied customers generate ongoing sales. But how do you keep your customers happy after the initial sale is made?

THE SECRET TO CUSTOMER SATISFACTION

The secret to keeping your customers satisfied is this: Don't just give them their money's worth—give them MORE than their money's worth. As Jerry Hardy, publisher of Time-Life Books, puts it: "Our policy will be to give the customer more than he has any right to expect."

Giving your customers more than their money's worth involves two steps:

- Creating realistic expectations
- Consistently exceeding expectations and delivering more than promised

Creating Realistic Expectations

Most salespeople promise more than they can deliver. But to achieve a superior level of satisfaction among your customers, you should deliver more than you promise. To do this, you must offer an excellent product and extraordinary service. And you must underpromise rather than overpromise.

In today's highly competitive business environment, under-promising is a tricky thing. Underpromise too much, and you won't appear as good as other companies who are promising your customers much more.

On the other hand, promising no more and no less than you are capable of giving, and then giving it, won't make you any enemies, but it won't turn the customer into a fan for life either.

As for overpromising, you know what happens when you overpromise and then fail to deliver.

The key is to make promises to customers that are both attractive and accommodating, yet at the same time credible and realistic.

For example, let's say you provide a certain type of service. Your service is superior, and that puts you in heavy demand. As a result, normal turnaround time is five days.

A prospective customer comes to you via word of mouth. She wants to know what you can do for her, and how quickly you can do it. You promise a better outcome from your service than the competition provides, because you know that your service is superior and that your firm almost always does a better job. So far, so good.

Next is the issue of delivery. For this customer, five days is too long. Her firm represents a big, potentially very lucrative account, and she is asking for overnight turnaround.

The immediate temptation is to promise your customer anything to get the work and then hope she'll forgive you when you miss a deadline, because at that point you'll already have her business and she won't want to switch. Wrong. There's no faster route to losing business today than to create a dissatisfied customer. And there's no surer way to create a dissatisfied customer than failing to meet a deadline or live up to some other promise you've made.

So what do you do? In this case, the best thing might be a very frank discussion of the situation. You explain that while you want to help and give her the benefit of your superior service, the kind of quality you provide cannot be rendered overnight.

Tell the customer the real, specific reasons why this is so. For example, you do certain quality checks that other vendors don't, and this takes extra time. You would prefer not to eliminate quality checks, because of your reputation for doing superior work.

Also, probe the customer's request. Does the work really have to be done overnight? What happens if it's done in two or three days instead of the the one day she is requesting? Often you find that customer demands are artificial—that is, the customer has set a particular deadline or created a specification without any real thought to whether it's necessary or not. In nine out of ten cases, you find there is no real event or other concrete deadline driving the "rush" job and that absolutely nothing would happen if it were done a day or a week later.

By having this type of discussion with the customer, you get her to see that not only are there legitimate reasons why the job shouldn't be done overnight, but also that it doesn't need to be anyway.

Still, five days is too long. She says, "What can you do for us?"

Here is where you put the "art of underpromising" to work. You've agreed that one day is too soon, five days too long. You know, but do not say, that you could comfortably do the work in three days but could also turn it around in two days, if need be. The customer says she would really love to have it in two days but could live with three.

The right move is to promise three-day turnaround. The customer has indicated she can accept this, and because you've already established that your service is technically superior, she'll likely go with you on a three-day basis.

Now you have created a situation where the customer has come to accept and agree to a three-day turnaround. It's not ideal, but it's been proposed and accepted. So now she expects to get it in three days. This puts you in a perfect position to deliver more than is expected because, as we've said, you can do the work in two or three days.

Tell her the first job will be ready in three days and then aim to deliver in two days. If you succeed, you will have exceeded the customer's expectation, resulting in a pleasantly surprised buyer. If you fail to meet your internal, self-imposed two-day deadline (a deadline the customer is unaware of), only you will know it, and the customer will still get the order in three days, ensuring that no external deadlines are missed.

By now you see the method: You promote all the superior aspects of the service you are going to deliver, while slightly underpromising on a single aspect. Then, when you do better than expected in this area, you exceed expectations and create extraordinary levels of customer satisfaction.

Give Your Customers More Than They Expect

At this point you may object, saying, "All well and good. But if the customer is paying for a Chevy, and I deliver a Rolls-Royce, it's costing me extra money. Sure, if I deliver much more than I promised the customer will be happy, but I won't make any money—and I'm in business to make a profit."

The solution is simple and straightforward: You can create an extraordinarily high level of pleasure and satisfaction in your customers by delivering only a *little* more than you promised, not much more. That's why giving your customers more than they have a right to expect need not cost you a lot in money, time, or effort.

The extras you provide don't have to be big. A simple gesture, a common courtesy, a faster response, a quicker completion time, handling a complaint or special request politely—these are the small things that make the customer's satisfaction soar and bond them to you for a long and happy relationship. Here are some techniques you can use.

1. Give Customers an Unexpected Free Gift with Their Order.

I recently bought several gift items in a local candy store. After packing my purchase, the clerk handed me a small box of chocolates taken from a basket on the counter. "What's this?" I asked.

"It's a free gift box of chocolates for you," she replied cheerily. "We give it as a gift to every customer who buys twenty dollars' worth of candy or more."

Important to note: The free gift had not been promised. There was no sign in the store advertising it, nor had it been featured in newspaper ads. Therefore, giving it had the added impact of surprise: It was a totally unanticipated and unexpected pleasure.

Had I come in response to an ad offering "free gift box with any $20 purchase," I wouldn't have been excited about getting the box; after all, it would have been what I expected to get. Perhaps I would have even been disappointed, thinking, "Gee, I came all this way for such a small box?" But the fact it was not promised assured my satisfaction. I had expected nothing and was getting something.

Want to create delighted customers? Try a free gift. It can be given with purchase or just to every customer who calls that week. The gift need not be elaborate. Indeed, the more unexpected it is, the less costly it need be to make the customer happy with it.

2. Be Accessible.

In today's fast-paced electronic age, many businesspeople use modern technology to juggle their busy schedules and put up barriers between themselves and their customers so they can manage what limited time they have more effectively. Problem is, while this practice may be convenient for you, your customers hate it.

Customers want to deal with vendors who are accessible and will take their calls. They want to feel that their calls are welcome, not an annoyance. They want to believe that their concerns and problems are your concerns and problems, not an intrusion into your already crammed schedule or busy day.

Many of us, pressured by too much to do and not enough time to do it, often seem agitated or distracted to our customer when we get calls from them. That's understandable, but not good: It annoys customers and puts them off. You may think seeming incredibly busy is a status symbol, but your customers think you're just showing off and that you are more concerned with your other business than with their orders or problems. And that's bad.

Also, some businesspeople behave hypocritically with their customers: They are always friendly, "up," and available when making the sale, but as soon as the contract is signed, all the customer hears is "He's not at his desk right now; I'll take a message." The customer senses the hypocrisy in this and is rightly offended. "I was important to you when you wanted my business," the customer thinks. "Now that you've got it, you're too busy wooing other customers to return my calls."

Although they do not like this behavior, customers have come to expect it. So when you are more accessible than your customer expects—friendlier, more helpful, quick to take and return calls—they become relaxed and happy. "At last here's someone who treats me right," they think, and this elevates you in status head and shoulders above the other vendors they deal with.

How can you be more accessible? One possibility might be to answer your own phone or, if that's not feasible, at least to reduce the amount of "grilling" callers are subjected to before your assistant puts them through to you. Other ideas: Give your customers your home number. Have an answering machine or voice-mail system take calls after hours, and check for messages once or twice a night and on weekends. Wear a beeper.

3. Fulfill Requests Promptly and Politely.

This is the equivalent of "shock therapy" in business: It jolts the customer into awareness because it's so sudden and unexpected. The customer has come to anticipate poor attitudes, poor service, impolite assistance, and slow, impersonal response. When you do what customers ask promptly and politely, they're shocked and delighted. When a customer wants to get a price quote, order a spare part, ask a question, or check product availability, he or she wants a fast answer that is both accurate and courteous.

The combination of promptness and politeness is critical. An exceptional effort made on the customer's behalf isn't enough to win her loyalty in the fickle, customer-driven business environment of the 1990s and beyond. To create exceptional customer satisfaction, not only must you do whatever the customer asks, but you also must do it quickly and with a smile on your face.

Customers will not appreciate your efforts if you are slow,

because they are impatient and hate to wait. They also will be put off if there is anything in your tone, manner, or behavior that suggests you are annoyed or unhappy about their request.

4. Correct Problems Promptly and Politely.

Although you have certain policies that limit how far you'll go or how much you'll give in when dealing with customers, you should probably suspend most or all of these limitations when a problem arises.

Today's high-demand customers are totally intolerant of problems, expect you to do what they ask when they ask it, and will not continue to do business with a vendor who says, "Sorry, but I can't help you."

When a problem arises, acknowledge it, apologize for it, and then move quickly to focus on the solution. Do everything you can to correct it. And do so quickly and politely.

Did you ever ask a barber, waitress, repair person, or retailer to fix or change something that was not quite to your liking and have them start arguing with you? If so, you know that the worst thing you can do with customers who are dissatisfied is to give them a hard time. When customers have a problem, they need to see immediately that you are on their side and dedicated to resolve it.

Even better than correcting problems quickly and courteously is to do it without charging the customer, even if there would be just cause for you to charge them.

We have a contractor who has done three remodeling jobs for us and will soon do a fourth. His work is excellent; his prices are competitive but certainly not the cheapest. The main reason we will use him again, however, is that when he is in our home, he frequently goes through the house and fixes minor things and never bills us for this. Even when we asked him to do a few simple repair jobs that did not involve things he had originally built for us, he did them (or had his assistant do them) and in most instances did not charge us.

You can imagine how delighted I was not only with this willingness to help us out but also with his invoice. The charges for the remodeling jobs were big enough as it was; it was certainly a pleasure not to have another few hundred dollars tacked on for the odd jobs he had handled. Obviously, if I had asked him to do something very time-consuming, he would have billed me and I would gladly have paid it. But by giving me an extra hour of his time and labor free now and then, he has gotten repeat business from me worth more than $55,000.

5. *Compensate Customers for Their Trouble.*

You can prevent customers from becoming dissatisfied by correcting problems quickly and courteously. You can put a smile on their faces by not charging them for it. But you'll really cement your relationship and build extraordinary loyalty by paying them for their time and trouble.

In effect, this says to the customer: We believe that when you pay for our service, you have every right to be satisfied at all times. If there is a problem and you become dissatisfied, this is our fault, and not only will we do everything in our power to correct the defect quickly and efficiently, without charge to you, but we will also compensate you for your "pain and suffering."

You can "pay" the customer through a refund or rebate on the invoice owed, but this isn't the best strategy. For one thing, it visibly reminds the customer of the problems involved on this job. For another, it costs you cash—unnecessarily, in my view—so that you have a loss instead of a profit.

A better way to compensate the customer is to offer a credit, discount, fee reduction, or other cost savings on his next order. This is a better choice for you because:

- The customer will be pleased and happy with such an offer.

- It shows fairness on your part.
- You still get your fee for the current job, so you don't feel upset or angry about the incident (as you would if you didn't get paid in full).
- You have now created a strong incentive for the customers to use you again for their next project because they have a credit with you that they don't benefit from until they actually retain you and apply the credit toward your fee on the new job.

So giving a credit or discount on future service is not only a good way to resolve today's problem in a manner that makes the customer happy, but also a selling technique for making sure you get the next job from him as well.

Cliffside Industries, a hardware distributor, has a standard sales letter that goes out anytime there is a problem with an order. The letter apologizes for the problem and offers the customer a discount ranging from 20 to 40 percent or more on the next order they place.

6. Follow Up Unexpectedly at Least Once.

A major mistake is communicating with your customers only when necessary or only when they expect to hear from you.

Although we don't realize it, our customers are sometimes not as confident in buying from us as we may think. Perhaps they were burned in the past by a vendor who did not deliver as promised. So although they are giving you a try, they may be a little nervous about it, a little worried that their negative past experience may be repeated.

Communication between vendor and customer is the solution. When customers call, act happy to hear from them, not annoyed. Treat their calls as a sales and customer service opportunity, not an interruption. Use the call to build a positive relationship with the customer. Don't, as so many do, act as if the customer is "bothering" you. How can she be bothering you when she is paying you, and the primary reason your company exists is to serve your customers?

Taking it one step further, don't wait for customers to call you and ask, "How's the project going?" Pick up the phone and call them before they expected to hear from you. Say hello, touch base, and give them a quick update on the project's progress. Customers appreciate this far more than you can imagine. It shows that you are concerned not only with the job but with their personal or professional stake in having you do the job well.

For consumers, how well you perform is important because it can affect their quality of life and because the money is coming out of their own pockets. For business customers, how well you perform determines how their supervisors and superiors will judge them. If you fail to deliver, people will say they made a poor decision in buying from you. If you do well, your performance makes them look good to their management.

Therefore, hearing from you is reassuring to your customers; it makes them feel better to know that everything is going smoothly and their order or project is on schedule.

If there is too lengthy a period between customer contacts, the customer who feels compelled to phone and ask "How's it going?" is already experiencing mild anxiety and nervousness. You want your customers to feel relaxed and confident, not nervous and jumpy. So don't wait for them to call. Call them first.

7. Pay Personal Attention to Each Customer.

You have a business relationship with your customers, and you can strengthen that business relationship by establishing a personal relationship as well. This does not mean that you need to become personal friends with customers or let socializing with customers impinge on your personal life. All it requires is to "be human"—to attend to the customer as a human being as well as a buyer of goods and services.

The best way to accomplish this is by rapport achieved through small talk. Find some common ground between you and the customers and let that be the icebreaker that makes them think of you as a person, and not just a "consultant" or "contractor" or whatever it is you do.

You will find that, even if you and the customer are very different and would not be compatible as friends, there is almost always some common ground that can be used to strengthen the bond between you. This might be sports, family, hobbies, likes or dislikes, similarities in lifestyle, or any one of a number of things. Avoid discussing sex, religion, money, and politics.

8. Offer the Customer Something Special.

For example, if you're an antiques dealer and you come across a piece of beautiful carnival glass that's a real find yet reasonably priced, call your customer who collects carnival glass and offer it to her first before you display it for your walk-in trade.

If you're an innkeeper and you're planning special activities and fantastic meals for a particular season or holiday, send a postcard to your "house list" of past lodgers inviting them to this special event. If they bring the postcard with them or mention it when making phone reservations, they get $25 off.

If you sponsor public conferences or seminars, send a personal letter of invitation to past attendees of previous years' programs before your regular mailing goes out, and offer these past attendees a special "alumni discount."

You create extraordinary customer satisfaction when you convey the impression that even when you're not currently under contract or rendering service to that customer, you're always on the lookout for things he or she would want or that can be of help. Send publications, articles, and books of interest. Customers appreciate that you are thinking of them and doing so with no immediate profit motive in mind.

Spend one hour every week thinking of new ideas and ways to help your customers. This is an unpaid hour, above and beyond what they are already buying from you. Customers will be delighted you are working so hard on their behalf. Many will buy one or more of the ideas you suggest, adding handsomely to the year's sales.

9. Give Extra Product or Service.

Several years ago, we made a pleasant discovery: a good restaurant in New York City that gives free seconds on any dish at any time. This policy costs them very little, since few patrons take advantage of it (regular portions are more than adequate). But it makes them memorable and sets them apart from their numerous competitors—in some areas of Manhattan there are two to three restaurants or more on virtually every block in the neighborhood.

This "free seconds" idea can also be applied, with a slight variation, to ensuring customer satisfaction in your business. The basic principle is this: When selling a certain item to customers, include some additional product or follow-up service that they can choose to use or not, at their option, included free with the original purchase.

For example, a friend of mine gives training seminars to corporations on business communications. He says to customers, "If any of the people you send to my seminar find they need more help or want more information, they can call my Business Communication Telephone Hotline during the next thirty days for assistance—and, because they are alumni of my program, there will be no charge for me to consult with them or answer their questions."

This variation of "free seconds" adds to the perceived value of my friend's training programs and also to his credibility. Not only is he giving more value for the money than seminar providers whose fees include the training session only with no follow-up privileges, but also he is in effect guaranteeing that trainees will genuinely get the knowledge they need when he is hired, since he will answer their questions long after the seminar is over.

This added level of service helps differentiate him from his competitors and has accounted for part of his tremendous success in the training field. Interestingly, while many new customers comment on how much they appreciate getting the use of the hotline included with their training courses, very few attendees actually use it. So it costs him very little in time to offer this valuable extra.

This method is extremely effective as a "sales closer," especially when selling additional services to existing customers. Let's say the customer is indecisive or unconvinced as to whether the fee you are asking for the service you are providing is justified. Probably there is not a huge gap between what you are asking and what the customer is comfortable paying; more likely, you would have to do only a "little better" to make the customer feel comfortable with the value he is getting.

Instead of lowering the price, you say to the customer, "Okay, I tell you what: Hire us today to do X and we'll also give you Y and Z at no charge." X is the main job; Y and Z are small related or ancillary tasks that take very little time but have a high perceived value to the customer. When the customer feels he is getting three services—X, Y, and Z—and you are charging only for X, he grows comfortable with your price and the level of service you are providing for that fee, which in turn helps build overall customer satisfaction.

Sometimes, even if you don't absolutely have to, it's better to give the customer a little extra service or, conversely, charge a bit less. Just because the customer signed your contract doesn't mean she feels comfortable with it; perhaps she signed because of imminent deadlines or other pressing needs, but feels that you are ripping her off and are taking advantage of her situation by charging too much for too little. You may indeed be making a high profit on that job, but are you building customer satisfaction and a long-term relationship based on maintaining that satisfaction?

Any contract you get a customer to sign should be a win-win situation for you and the customer. Giving a little extra service or a small "freebie" is a simple way to overcome customer resistance or displeasure and create a customer who's comfortable with the deal and feels you are being more than fair—generous, even. "The challenge is to deliver results that exceed the customer's expectations," writes Paul Vaughn, chairman of Hooven Direct Mail. "Providing customers with a service they hadn't expected is an excellent customer-retention strategy."

10. Charge Slightly Less Than the Original Estimate or Purchase Order.

Most surprises customers get are unpleasant: a botched job, a job that was not done as ordered, a missed deadline. So it makes an enormous impression on your customers when you give them a pleasant surprise.

One easy way to do this is to send an invoice that is slightly less than the original estimate. Most vendors seek to do exactly the opposite. Reason: As the job progresses, and they have to do the actual work, they realize how much effort is involved and that they probably bid too low to get the job.

So they get "revenge" on the customer by charging for every little expense, for every change in customer direction, for every little extra service that was provided along the way. The result is a bill 10 to 20 percent or more higher than the original estimate. One magazine editor recently complained that a freelance writer he hired to do a story charged him for the cost of the fax paper when he sent background material to her via fax!

The problem? Customers dislike receiving bills higher than they budgeted for or contracted for. Everyone, both the consumer and the business buyer, is on a budget today. Going over budget hurts consumers because it's money out of their pocket. And it hurts business buyers because it makes them look bad to their management.

A colleague of mine who owns a small ad agency told me she had hired a freelance graphic artist to do some design work. The artist bills $50 per hour. My colleague loved his work, but when she got the bill from him, there was a $50 charge for one hour for showing her his portfolio and presenting his services and capabilities to her! This was completely unexpected—"I didn't expect to be billed for his sales presentation to me"—and started the relationship off on a negative tone instead of an upbeat one.

You can be different by sending the customer an invoice for an amount equal to or, even better, slightly less than your estimate. Your invoice should show clearly the amount of the discount, both in dollars and percentage savings, as well as the reason for the discount—e.g., you spent fewer hours than anticipated, or the cost of materials was lower, or the parts required less machining than estimated, or you didn't have to do a certain phase or step you thought you would have to do when you gave the original estimate.

Customers will see that you were able to achieve a cost reduction and then, instead of keeping it as extra profit, passed the cost savings directly on to them through a lower charge.

Taking a few dollars off an invoice now and then won't cost you a fortune, and there are few things as effective as a slight reduction in the final bill that will give your customers such a pleasant surprise or make them think of you as favorably as this will. It builds your credibility and it's much appreciated.

11. Complete the Job Slightly Faster Than the Original Deadline.

Next to getting it done cheaper, getting it done sooner is the thing that will "knock the socks" off your customer. Everybody is in a hurry nowadays. If the original deadline is tight, beating it will make your customer that much happier. If the original deadline is distant, the customer will appreciate the extra time to review your work or use what you provide if you get it to her a week earlier.

Be careful, though: Do not complete the work too early. The danger is that you might give customers the impression that you rushed their job, didn't give it your best effort, and therefore did an inadequate job. As a rule of thumb, if you are going to deliver your work or complete the job early, don't beat the deadline by more than 20 to 25 percent.

12. Keep Complete, Well-organized Records—and Have Them at Your Fingertips.

Nothing annoys customers more when they call you up and ask you a question than for you to say, "Gee, I don't know" or "I have no idea."

We live in an age of instant information, a time when people are impatient with anything less than an immediate response to their queries. For this reason, many large companies have spent hundreds of thousands of dollars on computer and communications systems designed to help customer-service people gain fast access to customer records, track projects, respond to inquiries, and resolve problems.

For the one-person office and other small businesses, you can achieve the equivalent by keeping well-organized and complete files on each job, and storing those files in a place where you have quick and easy access to them.

If a customer calls with a question or problem dealing with a current or past job, you should be able to access the information immediately while the customer is on the phone—or at least be able to find it so that you can call back with some answers or to discuss the problem within the next five minutes. Keeping a frustrated or annoyed customer waiting for preliminary answers longer than that creates an impression of poor service and incompetence. Customers like to know you are in control of your information, are well organized, and have designed your office procedures to respond quickly to their needs.

In addition to keeping well-organized files, you can use your personal computer to put important customer information within easy reach. Some people use popular database software to maintain customer information; others use personal information managers or customer contact management programs more specific to their needs (see page 136).

Having the proper information immediately available when customers call with a query or complaint puts them at ease and creates a professional image for your business. Being unable to find the relevant documents when customers call frustrates them and creates a negative impression. The longer you force customers to wait for an answer to a question or a response to a problem, the more dissatisfied they will become.

13. Don't Be a Prima Donna.

In the salad days of the 1980s, many businesses could afford to indulge their egos to a degree and act like prima donnas. In those days, if you were a skilled craftsperson, carpenter, contractor, mason, photographer, graphic artist, software developer, or whatever, the demand for your services was probably greater than the supply, which meant you could call your own shots, be choosy about the customers you accepted, and casual, even gruff, in the way you dealt with and treated your customers.

Customers would put up with prima donna vendors because they were willing to endure the less than exemplary treatment to gain access to the skills and services of these vendors. But that doesn't mean they liked being treated poorly or indifferently.

The recession of the early 1990s permanently changed the situation. When buyers stopped spending, vendors, instead of having customers lined up and waiting to buy, had to go out and ask for work—almost beg for it, in some cases—to keep their businesses solvent. Customers saw that they, not the vendors, were in control: The vendor needs the customer's money, but the customer can probably live without the vendor's product by going elsewhere. As a result, a lot of vendors in many fields who were prima donnas are prima donnas no longer. Now they are humble laborers, competing with many firms providing similar goods and services for a shrinking number of applications as customers cut back or do it themselves.

Being a prima donna was once an effective image for vendors in that it made them look busy, important, and in demand. But in today's "age of the customer," this image approach doesn't work.

The bottom line: Don't be a prima donna. Customers want to work with vendors who are friendly and accessible and who have their egos in check.

Today, customers have no patience with and no need for snobs. You may think you're an original and that being standoffish only makes you more desirable to the customers. In one case in a million that may be true, but for the majority, being a prima donna will bump you off the short list of vendors being considered for the job.

BE DILIGENT ABOUT OFFERING SUPERIOR CUSTOMER SERVICE

If you've already put these principles to work and are getting good results, you may think, "Things are pretty okay with my customers at this point; now I can relax." Not so. One of the key secrets of ensuring customer satisfaction is *diligence:* keeping at it week after week, month after month, for as long as you are in business.

Customer satisfaction is not something you practice one

month, then coast on when things are going smoothly. It is an attitude, and a way of doing business, that must be diligently applied every waking moment, every minute of the business day.

It takes months, even years, of excellent customer service to form solid, lasting relationships with the most profitable, lucrative customers. And all that can be destroyed with one slip, one mistake, one lapse, one error that gets the customers ticked off at you enough to make them walk. Therefore, you can't "relax" when it comes to applying the principles of maximum customer satisfaction expressed in this chapter. You have to do it every week, every day, every hour, every minute. Tiring? Possibly. Doable? Yes. Rewarding? I guarantee it.

Another reason why diligently practicing maximum customer satisfaction and never letting down your guard is important is that in this age of the customer, only the firms that create maximum customer satisfaction will survive and prosper.

"Let's make sure that our customers are satisfied," suggests Lois Geller, president of Lois Geller Direct, in an article in *Target Marketing*. "Lack of customer service can break all of our efforts. If we are to cement buyer loyalty in the nineties, customer satisfaction must be a key objective."

Low levels of customer satisfaction can cost your business a lot of money. According to the investment consultant and author John M. Cali, Jr., 91 percent of unhappy customers who have been treated discourteously will not buy from the offending business again unless deliberate steps are taken to get them back. And just as bad, says Cali, is that the average unhappy customer will complain about the poor treatment they received from you to 9 or 10 other people, and 13 percent of these unhappy customers will tell more than 20 other people!

According to the American Productivity and Quality Center:

- Sixty-eight percent of customers stop doing business if they receive poor service.

- Customers are five times more likely to leave because of poor service than because of product quality or cost.
- Losing a customer costs five times the annual value of the customer account.
- The average happy customer tells five other people.
- Fifty to 75 percent of customers who have their complaints solved quickly return and buy again.

Differentiate Yourself from the Competition

Many business authorities say the only way to succeed is by being great at everything you do. The book *In Search of Excellence* inspired a new breed of business authors, speakers, and seminar leaders proclaiming that only "excellence" will win customers and profits in the 1990s.

While striving for excellence is a laudable goal, there are two problems I have with experts telling you that you have to be great or excellent to stay in business. First, it puts tremendous pressure on you. It's hard enough today to juggle all your customer responsibilities and still get all your work done on time. To have to be great in *everything you do* as well? It's too much!

Second, it's not true. You see, to stand head and shoulders above your competition, you don't have to be "great" or "excellent," you just have to be significantly *better* than the competition.

In giving excellent customer service, that's fairly easy, because despite all we read in the business press about the importance of customer service, most businesses are not all that great when it comes to customer service. So you don't have to be great; you just have to be better than they are. And because they're so mediocre, it's easy for you to beat them.

"You beat 50 percent of the people in America by working hard," says A. L. Williams, the self-made millionaire life insurance salesman, in his book, *All You Can Do Is All You Can Do.* "You beat another 40 percent by being a person of honesty and integrity and by standing for something. The last 10 percent is a dogfight in the free enterprise system."

Listen to Your Customers

Failure to listen is usually caused by eagerness to speak. When you find yourself cutting off the other person's sentences, or not listening but sitting there waiting for her to finish so you can talk, you're not really listening. And that's bad for two reasons.

First, if you don't listen, you don't know what the customer really wants you to do; therefore, you can't do it. And if you don't do what the customer wants, you don't have a satisfied customer.

Second, it annoys the customer. If she senses you are not listening, she will feel you are not interested in her and her problems.

Equally as important as listening is *to let the customer know you* are listening. This can be accomplished with brief verbal responses that show you are paying attention ("I understand"; "That's interesting"; "Really?"; "Uh-huh"; "Tell me more"). Another useful technique is to pause for a full second or two before you begin your reply after the customer is done speaking.

If you jump in too soon, the customer may get the false impression that you weren't really listening and were just waiting for your turn to speak. By pausing for a second or two, you convey the impression that you have listened carefully and are still formulating your response.

Give your customers your full attention and all the time they need. Be efficient, but don't let them feel they are being rushed. Have incoming calls routed to voice mail or a secretary so your conversations with customers aren't interrupted.

Customers today perceive they are in a buyer's market. They know they can switch vendors, and it takes little aggravation or unhappiness to prompt them to look into doing so. Selling wins the first order, but service is just as important as selling—perhaps even more so—in securing repeat orders, year after year. And that's the best way to build a profitable business in today's customer-focused marketplace.

Thirteen

Add-on Sales

If you have followed the instructions and practiced the techniques in this book and have applied them according to the telephone sales plan you created in chapter 4, you should be well on your way to achieving your sales quota and income objective.

This brief chapter gives you four simple techniques for exceeding your target sales quota by 10 to 20 percent or more *without* changing your plan or increasing the number of daily cold calls you make. These techniques are: referrals, repeat business, upgrading, and upselling.

Using the Telephone to Generate Referrals

Earlier in this book we developed scripts and techniques for picking up the phone and calling a potential customer cold from a telemarketing list, directory, or other source.

As you know, you will get much higher "hit" rates when you call lists of people who have been referred to you than if you use outside lists. After all, which is more powerful:

"My name is Brian Jones, and I'm with XYZ Business Services" or

"My name is Brian Jones. I'm with XYZ Business Services. Joe Blow at QRS Company gave me your name and suggested I give you a call."

Obviously, if the prospect knows Joe and respects him, he'll be more inclined to listen to the second call.

If calls to referrals generate better response than calls to cold prospects, you should be making more calls to referred leads.

How do you go about getting referrals? You do it by calling your best customers and asking them for referrals.

Although this can be a separate call, it's better if combined with a call for another purpose—to keep in touch, check on customer satisfaction, follow up on a service request, or check on an order. Here's how it might go:

YOU: Mike, can I ask you a question?

PROSPECT: Sure, go ahead.

YOU: You seem pretty satisfied with our product and our service. Am I right?

PROSPECT: Yes, we're very satisfied.

YOU: Would you be comfortable recommending our company to colleagues of yours who are not direct competitors with your firm?

PROSPECT: Of course.

YOU: Which of these people could I get in touch with to let them know about our product and service and how it can help him?

PROSPECT: Joe Doakes at Hummingbird Industries.

YOU: And do you have Joe's phone number?

PROSPECT: XXX-XXX-XXXX.

YOU: Joe Doakes at Hummingbird. May I use your name when I call him?

PROSPECT: Certainly.

YOU: Great. I'll call Joe. Who else do you know who might be able to benefit from our products and services?

You then repeat the cycle, ending with "Who else?" until the customer gives you all the referrals he or she is going to give you right now. By asking "Who else?" you will probably get two or three referrals instead of the one the customer was going to give you. Three is probably the limit for one call—the customer will run out of ready names and get tired of giving the referrals—but ask until she says, "That's it."

I recommend you send a thank-you note to customers who give you referrals. A small, tasteful gift is optional. (I send a copy of one of my books.)

Keep the customer up to date if anything comes from the referral. If you get business out of it, send another thank-you and a slightly better gift (my choice is a gift basket of muffins from Wolferman's: 800-999-1910).

You can ask these same customers for more referrals later on, but don't do it too frequently. Once every four or five months seems about right. If you do something particularly good for them, such as solve a problem or complete a successful project, by all means ask for a reference as you bask in the glow of their praise.

USING THE TELEPHONE TO GENERATE REPEAT BUSINESS AND REORDERS

Salespeople tend to focus on pursuing new business, but there is a potentially more lucrative source of revenue you can exploit: getting additional orders from your existing customers.

Because many salespeople love the thrill of the chase, and because they often get bigger commissions for bringing in new customers, soliciting repeat sales and reorders from active accounts is often ignored at the expense of pursuing new business.

Not every teleseller makes this mistake. Stockbrokers, for example, know the value of working existing accounts. If you have an account with a brokerage firm, you get frequent calls from your broker offering new ideas for companies he wants you to invest in. But tellers in some other industries are not as savvy. For example, the company that sold me my computer has never contacted me to offer any upgrades or new services, despite the fact there are many they have that I would want—a bigger memory, a better CD-ROM drive, a higher-resolution laser printer, or home page design. A mistake? I think so.

Have a plan for periodically recontacting active customers to remind them of your existence and give them news of any special offers, discounts, new products, or new services they might benefit from. Doing so will substantially increase reorders and repeat sales from your database of existing clients.

Experience shows that an active customer is five to ten times more likely to buy something from you than a prospect you cold-call from a prospecting directory or telemarketing list. That means "working your database" can yield five to ten times the response of a new business or customer acquisition effort aimed at a similar number of prospects.

How frequently should you keep in touch with existing customers? It's different for every business, but for many small companies, a contact every quarter—a call or mailing once every three months, for a total of four in a given year—makes sense. It's frequent enough so the customer doesn't forget about you, but infrequent enough so that you're not pestering customers or spending an inordinate amount of time and money maintaining these contacts.

If possible, make most of the contacts phone calls. You can increase frequency of contact by adding one, two, or three mailings a year, or by substituting a mailing for one or two of the four annual phone calls. The mailing need not be elaborate. Remember, this is just to keep in touch and keep your name before the customer. A simple postcard or short sales letter are more than sufficient.

Using the Telephone to Upgrade

I heard the following story at a business meeting, and since I know the person who told it to be an honest and reputable consultant in the selling and marketing fields, I believe it to be true.

One of the nation's largest software companies decided to do a massive telephone survey of its thousands of customers. The purpose was to update the database and conduct research that would be useful in future marketing campaigns. Thus these were not sales calls, in the sense that no product or service was being offered.

The timing of this massive phone campaign coincided with the nationwide release of the latest version of this firm's popular PC software.

The consultant I spoke of, who was working with this firm, made this simple suggestion to the marketing director: "When you finish the survey, mention that the upgrade is now available at a list price of $99. Offer to send it to the prospect, in appreciation of their completing the survey, for only $29 if they give you their credit-card information over the phone right then and there." The program worked phenomenally well, generating millions of dollars in additional revenues at virtually zero marketing cost.

The telephone can be used for selling upgrades, enhancements, accessories, options, new models, add-ons, and other additions and improvements to an existing product, system, or service.

Here are some quick tips on upgrade selling via telephone:

• The key is to position the upgrade call as a customer service call rather than a sales call. For instance, instead of saying, "We are calling to sell you something," say, "We are introducing a new and improved version of the XYZ system. I am calling today to offer it to you as an existing system owner at a fifty percent discount off the retail rate."

• If you are offering the upgrade or enhancement at cost, or at a slight profit margin, tell the prospect your company is making this offer as a service to help the prospect, and that you are not making a profit on the deal or are making only a nominal profit to cover time and labor, development costs, and so on.

• Sell the upgrade as a long-awaited solution designed in response to customer demand, if this indeed is the case. Many companies develop upgrades in response to customer complaints, requests, and wishes. If you have done this, position the upgrade as something the customers and their fellow users have asked for and been waiting for. Then offer it at a big "preferred customer" discount.

• Sell the benefit of the upgrade. If the upgrade is something you invented because you think it's a good idea, and not because customers were asking for it, stress the new features and capabilities and the benefits and advantages these features will give the user. After talking up the benefit, mention how easy it is to get the product by saying yes now over the phone, and stress the big discount you are offering.

• Sometimes an upgrade makes previous models or versions obsolete. Or future enhancements will be compatible only with the upgrade and not the original model. Or technical support will be available only for the upgrade, not the old version.

If this is the case, gently let the customer know it. Be mindful of the fact that some users may resent your making their version obsolete and "forcing" them to buy the latest model. So talk about all the benefits and improvements, and how their life will be better when they own the upgrade. But do make clear the limitations they will face if they stick with the old model and do not upgrade. Also stress that the current offer is the best discount you may ever offer for the new model, so they should act now to take advantage of it and save money.

USING THE TELEPHONE TO UPSELL

"Upsell" means to convince the prospect to buy more product or service than you originally offered or than he or she originally intended or agreed to purchase.

Take the example of a mail-order company that sells gourmet food. A customer gets the catalogue. She calls to order several food baskets to be sent as gifts. After taking the order the telephone representative says, "We are having a special today on a beautiful holiday minibasket that makes the perfect complement to a Christmas table. Because you are a first-time customer, you get twenty percent off if you order now." The representative describes the delicious foods in the basket, and the customer orders the item for herself. If the gift total was $80, and the charge for the holiday basket was $12 ($15 less the 20 percent discount), the telephone representative, within the space of 15 seconds and with virtually no extra selling effort, has increased the total order 15 percent.

Another example: A consumer buys a personal computer over the telephone. As the customer representative takes the order, he says, "Your XYZ computer comes with a ninety-day warranty on parts and labor. If there is a problem, ship it to us and we will repair or replace the defect free of charge. A full year's service contract including parts and labor, with repair at one of our depots, normally costs $120. If you order a service contract now, the cost will be only $90. For an additional $20, or only $110 total, we will upgrade the contract to an on-site service agreement, which will cover parts and labor for one full year of on-site repair, meaning we will send a technician to your home to make the repair at no extra cost. Would you prefer the off-site or on-site service option?" The sale is made quickly and easily, with no separate marketing effort required.

As you can see, upselling makes sense for telephone sellers. It takes almost no time. There is no added sales or marketing cost. And it can significantly raise your gross telephone sales without adding telephone sellers, lines, or stepping up activity. Companies that upsell when closing a sale or taking an incoming order can easily increase their gross sales by 10 to 20 percent or more. And the additional revenue is almost all profit.

Here are some tips for effective upselling:

• Have specials you can offer customers for your upsell efforts. Change the specials monthly, so there is always something new to offer.

• Offer customers add-ons. If someone is buying a vacuum cleaner over the phone, offer an extra attachment, extra supply of bags, or optional feature if he or she buys now.

• Discount the upsell item. The customers get the discount only when they accept the upsell right then and there, on the spot, as you are completing the transaction with them. After that, either the item is unavailable, or it is available but at its regular price with no discount.

• Service contracts and warranty extensions are a popular upsell. If you sell a $200 device with a 60-day warranty on parts and labor, offer a two-year service contract covering parts and labor for $35 more. If the customer doesn't take it now, the price should be more if ordered later.

• Offer financing. Say you finance a $10,000 product purchase with a four-year lease, and the monthly payment is $333. Now let's say you want to upsell the customer on a $1,000 add-on. Instead of the customer's paying $1,000 out of pocket, the upsell can be added to the lease and therefore offered to the customer at only an additional $41 per month.

• Combine upselling with other activities that require a telephone call to the customer. These include order confirmation, customer service, follow-up, billing or credit-card issues, delivery issues, warranty issues, subscription and policy renewals, special offers, surveys, and so on. The prospect is often more likely to accept the upsell if the call is not specifically made just for sales purposes; and you save money by eliminating the cost of making a separate call for the upsell offer.

☎ *Fourteen* ☎

The 17 Most Common Telephone Selling Mistakes and How to Avoid Them

So far in our discussion of teleselling, we have been talking mostly about the things you *should* be doing. Now let's review the things you should *not* be doing—errors that can turn prospects off, lose your sales, or waste your valuable time.

This chapter talks about the most common mistakes made when doing telephone sales—and how to avoid them. These mistakes include:

1. Not asking prospects if you are catching them at a bad time
2. Launching into a canned presentation before asking the prospect's permission to give your sales pitch
3. Being vague or evasive about who you are, what your company does, and why you are calling
4. Giving the prospect the impression you are reading a script
5. Not changing your tone or content in response to the prospect's reactions to what you've said
6. Telling prospects they are wrong or that they are making a mistake by not being interested
7. Telling prospects their objections—or they—are stupid

8. Arguing or fighting with your prospects
9. Trying to prove you are right
10. Getting defensive
11. Being arrogant
12. Not having a response to the prospect's objection or turn-down of your offer
13. Not bothering to uncover the prospect's real needs by asking questions
14. Not having a range of other options to offer prospects who turn down your primary offer
15. Refusing to mail or fax literature to real prospects with genuine information who ask to see something in writing
16. Forgetting to ask for referrals from prospects who turn you down
17. Not qualifying prospects up front.

Let's take a look at each item on the list. We'll discuss what it is, why it's bad, and how you can avoid doing it.

Teleselling Mistake 1: Not Asking Prospects If You Are Catching Them at a Bad Time

I have an unusual telephone technique that works extremely well for me. Whenever I call someone, whether it's a sales call or to discuss an ongoing project with a customer, the first thing I say after identifying myself is "Am I catching you at a bad time right now?" This is a magic phrase that can work wonders for you.

Most professional sales trainers would tell you never to say this. "After all," they'd explain, "this gives the prospect the opportunity to say 'yes' and get you off the phone?"

My response? I'd rather not try to sell something to a prospect who is too busy to talk. I prefer to speak to prospects when they have the time and inclination to discuss my services and products, which usually means there is an immediate, future, or potential need.

Have you ever talked with someone who obviously was busy and didn't want to be on the phone with you? It's a situation you want to avoid. Prospects take action according to their schedule primarily, not yours. Just because you have a good product—one the prospect could benefit from having—doesn't mean that now is the right time for him to talk about it.

Have you ever gotten a telemarketing call while on a tight deadline for work or while cooking dinner? How receptive were you to the call? Not very, I'll guess. And what was your reaction when the telemarketer kept talking, even though you said you didn't want to? This pushy, obnoxious behavior, which ignores the needs and wishes of the prospect, is what gives telephone selling a bad name and is the reason many people dread getting sales calls.

"Am I catching you at a bad time?" is effective for several reasons.

First, it shows prospects you respect them and their time. It says, "I'm not going to take any of your time on the phone unless you tell me it's okay to do so."

Second, it flatters the prospect. People are busy today, so much so that being ultrabusy has evolved into a status symbol of sorts. People take pride in working long hours, being frantically busy, having long to-do lists, and being surrounded by piles of papers. When you say, "Am I catching you at a bad time?" you are subtly saying, "You are probably very busy—but would you talk to me anyway?"

"Am I catching you at a bad time?" is, in my opinion, more powerful than the alternate version suggested to me by a professional salesperson: "Am I catching you at a good time?" This assumes the prospect is not busy, which today is unlikely, and says,

"You probably don't have anything better to do anyway than listen to my sales call."

Third, if the prospect says, "It's okay" or "Go ahead," she has in essence given you permission to begin the sales call. You can proceed with dignity and at your own pace, without feeling you have to rush because the prospect is tapping her foot impatiently at the other end of the phone line. She may be. But that's okay, because she has said to you, "I authorize you to proceed and I agree to listen."

Fourth, if the prospect says, "This is a bad time right now" or "Yes, I am very busy right now," you've found out what you wanted to know: that you have called at an inappropriate time and the prospect does not want to discuss the subject right now.

You should ask, "When would be a good day and time to call you back?" Most prospects will either give you a day and time or tell you to go ahead on the spot. A typical response is, "Can you tell me what this call is about?"—which is the equivalent of saying, "Start telling me what you want to tell me." Only a handful of prospects will not ask what the call is about and tell you not to call back ever.

Telesellers who insist on diving into their presentation regardless of the prospect's willingness or readiness to hear it are from the old school of selling. They believe prospects and salespeople are adversaries, and that they can somehow force you to listen and buy if they talk fast enough and don't allow you to interrupt. They are wrong, of course.

TELESELLING MISTAKE 2: LAUNCHING INTO A CANNED PRESENTATION BEFORE ASKING THE PROSPECT'S PERMISSION TO GIVE YOUR SALES PITCH

Certain books and courses teach that you should launch immediately into your sales pitch before the prospect realizes what you are doing and has a chance to interrupt you.

My approach is the opposite. At the beginning of the call, I want zero or minimal "selling" or sales pitch. As stated in chapter 6, I advocate using the "prospect need" opening. After asking a prospect whether now is a good time to talk, you ask questions to determine whether he or she is the right person to talk to and whether they have any interest in hearing about your product or service. You prequalify prospects to make sure they are the right people to talk with, and to see if there's any point in having the conversation. If you need a refresher in this opening, turn to chapter 6 and reread the section on the prospect need opening. Practice the script until you're comfortable with it. You'll find it to be more effective than the standard openings for most sales situations.

The prospect either knows or suspects that you are making a sales call. Since you are, there is no point in trying to mask it as something else. There are, however, ways of opening the call in an inoffensive manner that can get the prospect happily involved in a conversation.

One is to talk about a problem, rather than to start selling your product. Another is to talk about a benefit you offer. The third is to ask questions, as in the prospect need opening, to qualify the prospect. For example: "Are you the person in charge of buying widgets for your company?" and "What would it take for us to do business with your firm?"

Be aware of how you say things, as well as what you say. Sometimes phrases that seem logical come off with a phony or high-pressure ring if spoken too rapidly or too dramatically.

An example: Years ago, a teleseller called and asked me, "Mr. Bly, if I could show you how to save one to five thousand dollars or more a year on pocket folders, would you be interested in taking a look?"

This is a canned, scripted opening, and I suppose it can work. However, my response, which took the salesman aback, was "No, I would not be." Had he asked why, I would have told him I was not interested in discounts on pocket folders because, at the time, I didn't *use* pocket folders.

In such a situation, the prospect need opening is far more effective. Why not ask me first (1) if I am the person at our company responsible for buying printed promotional materials and (2) do we currently use pocket folders to send out materials to prospects? Once the prospect tells you the company uses pocket folders, then it makes sense to ask her whether they'd like to save thousands of dollars when buying the product. Without qualifying me first, the salesman came off as foolish or at least ignorant, and his well-rehearsed opening fell absolutely flat.

Teleselling Mistake 3: Being Vague or Evasive About Who You Are, What Your Company Does, and Why You Are Calling

I have attended sales training programs where the instructors said not to say what your company is or does directly, but to couch it in terms of benefits only. For instance, instead of saying, "We offer seminars on teamwork and leadership," say, "We help companies improve teamwork, leadership, and productivity." The idea is that telling exactly what you do (e.g., you're a seminar company, printer, word processing service) alerts prospects too early in the call to the fact that you are attempting to sell them something. Supposedly, dangling the benefit only (e.g., we help companies increase sales, save time, reduce costs), without revealing the specifics of how it is done will intrigue prospects and get them to ask you how you do it.

My experience is the opposite. Sometimes this benefits-only opening can work by intriguing prospects. But more often it annoys them and turns them off. Why?

The first things every prospect wants to know immediately are (1) your name, (2) your company, and (3) the reason for your call.

Not by coincidence, these are the three questions almost every receptionist and secretary asks you when you make cold calls. Others include "Does she know you?" and "Will she know what this is in reference to?" To attempt to hide your identity or mask the purpose of your call for anything more than a few seconds is folly and has a negative effect on your efforts.

On the other hand, there is some validity to the school that worries about being too up-front and revealing your hand too soon. "Hi, I'm Sam Jones from ColorExpress and I want to get your next printing job" is honest and forthright, but I'm not convinced it will work. The response I would expect: "We already have a printer and we are very happy with them."

The solution? A balance between the two approaches: Be specific about who you are and what your company does, but combine this, within the same opening, with a potential benefit or solution to a problem. In combination with the prospect need opening, it's an effective way of qualifying the prospect and introducing your company and its products. Here's how this might sound:

PROSPECT: Frank Carriello, marketing manager, speaking.
YOU: Mr. Carriello, this is Sam Jones calling. Am I catching you at a bad time?
PROSPECT: No, but can you tell me what this is about?
YOU: Sure. I'm Sam Jones with ColorExpress. We're a large four-color print shop that saves local companies up to thirty percent on their four-color print runs of one thousand pieces or more. Let me ask you, are you the person responsible for buying color printing at your company?
PROSPECT: I'm one of them.
YOU: And are you currently using color printers to produce pieces for you?
PROSPECT: We probably do one four-color piece every month or so.

YOU: If I could show you a way to maintain top quality while reducing your color printing bills ten to thirty percent or more, would you be interested in taking a look?

PROSPECT: Well, if you could do that, of course I'd be interested. But how can you charge less than your competitors?

YOU: [Answer the prospect's question here.]

Teleselling Mistake 4: Giving the Prospect the Impression That You Are Reading a Script

People want to deal with other people—not with corporations, not with machines, not with voice-mail systems, and certainly not with robots.

If you are not reading from a script, then you have little to worry about here. You may stumble, put in too many "uh"s or "um"s—but that makes you human. There's nothing wrong with being polished and in control, but its opposite—being human and natural—can help establish empathy with some prospects.

If you are forced to read from a script by your employer or client, here are a few tips that will make you sound more natural:

- Pay attention. Listen to prospects' responses. To let them know you are listening, pause briefly before responding with the appropriate scripted line.
- Do not speak in a monotone. Vary your tone and volume.
- Practice the script so many times that even though you have it in front of you, you can give the presentation and responses from memory.
- Ask your supervisor if it's okay to rephrase anything that

is particularly awkward for you (e.g., changing "it is" to "it's" because the contraction flows better in the script).

- Become a more polished speaker. Toastmasters, a public speaking organization, is a good place to start. To reach them call 800-993-7732.
- Pay attention to the telephone sales calls you get at work. Instead of cutting the callers off, let them finish, even if you are not interested in the product. Study the presentation. Make notes of what annoys you or doesn't work, and eliminate it from your own presentation.

TELESELLING MISTAKE 5: NOT CHANGING YOUR TONE OR CONTENT IN RESPONSE TO THE PROSPECT'S REACTIONS TO WHAT YOU'VE SAID

Example: If you say, "Hi, how are you today?" (not my favorite opening) and the prospect says "I'm not feeling well," don't go on to the next line of the script, which reads, "Great! I'm doing fine too!" Obviously it's inappropriate.

Human beings reflect emotions and feelings in their tone of voice. Some feelings and emotions—anger, disgust, annoyance, irritation—you want to conceal. But others—sympathy, happiness, warmth, caring, concern, curiosity—are an asset. So be a little "looser." Let your personality shine through in your voice. You'll enjoy the calls more and so will your prospects.

TELESELLING MISTAKE 6: TELLING PROSPECTS THEY ARE WRONG OR THAT THEY ARE MAKING A MISTAKE BY NOT BEING INTERESTED

The temptation is to argue with prospects: to tell them they are wrong, that they will suffer from choosing your competitor instead of you, that they clearly don't understand what they are doing if they are not buying *your* widgets, or that they will suffer or get in trouble as a result of their choice in the near future.

This type of sour grapes insults the prospect and gets you nowhere. People generally respect their own opinions and like to think themselves capable of making intelligent decisions—which they generally are. Also, you are a salesperson with a vested interest in having the prospect buy your product. So when you say the prospect is making a mistake buying the other vendor's products, it lacks credibility.

When prospects are leaning toward not making a purchase from you, there is still a chance to persuade them, as long as you reach them before they've committed to another supplier. Use the techniques outlined in this book, especially in chapter 8, "Cold Calls: The Objection Script." The argument that the prospects are making a mistake simply because they are not buying from you is weak. It lacks credibility, turns people off, and makes you look desperate.

If prospects have already made a decision and you were not selected as the vendor, don't criticize the product they bought. They think they made an intelligent decision and will resent any criticism of what is already a done deal. Instead, follow the advice in chapter 10, "Follow-up," and recontact these prospects when their evaluation of their newly purchased product or service is nearly complete, or when their contract is up for renewal. If they've had any problems with the vendor they chose, they'll be receptive to your call if you can show them a way to eliminate those problems by buying from you.

TELESELLING MISTAKE 7: TELLING PROSPECTS THEIR OBJECTIONS—OR THEY-ARE STUPID

This is similar to number 6 above, but more intense. I have occasionally had telesellers tell me in so many words that I was a dodo for not taking their recommendations. Or they say things so offensive they insult my intelligence. Although it should seem obvious, many tellesellers act as if they don't know that there is nothing to be gained by insulting the customer. This fundamental, commonsense rule is violated frequently, and it gives telephone selling a negative image.

Once when I was not responding positively to a sales pitch from a financial services telemarketer, he said to me, in a challenging, bold, almost adversarial tone of voice, "Mr. Bly, I don't understand. Do you object to making a profit?"

What a stupid question! As if anyone who is not smart enough to buy the stock he is selling today wants to lose money. I said, "Yes, I don't want to make a profit" and hung up.

As I've said, I get frequent calls from people trying to get me to invest in stocks. One told me it would be a mistake not to invest because the stock was certain to rise within the next three months. I said, "Tell me the price of the stock today. I will write it down but not buy it. Then call me in three months. If it has gone up as you say, I will try you on your next recommendation."

He told me, "Mr. Bly, in all my years as a stockbroker, that is the stupidest suggestion I have ever heard." Do you think he got my order?

Teleselling Mistake 8: Arguing or Fighting with Your Prospects

Do not argue or fight with your prospects. Since they are the ones writing the checks, it is an argument you cannot possibly win.

If there is a debate over how something should be done, your first suggestion should be your best recommendation, including what they should buy, the model they need, options, accessories, and how it should be installed. If they argue, politely review the advantages of your suggestion one time. If they still argue, then acquiesce pleasantly. Better to sell them a widget without the optional coat of varnish than no widget at all.

Sellers often complain to me, "But my customers are ignorant—they don't know what they are doing." My experience is that customers are not as ignorant as these sellers believe. Look at it from the customers' point of view. Is there a chance they could be right?

Also, once you have explained the consequences of the customers' decision to them, it is their right to make the choice, even if you consider the choice wrong. A recent article in the *New England Medical Journal* noted that even in health care, hospitalized patients deliberately refused physicians' recommended treatment about 10 percent of the time.

Today's customers are consumer activists. They feel they know what they're doing and like to make their own choices. The nearly godlike worship or authoritarian status people in some professions—doctors, teachers, police officers, contractors—once enjoyed has largely vanished. So when you say, "Our product is the best for you," customers are less likely to take you at your word today.

TELESELLING MISTAKE 9: TRYING TO PROVE YOU ARE RIGHT

In his book *In Search of Excellence,* Tom Peters observed, "People don't argue with their own data." Even though you may be correct, people take in information selectively. They tend to accept anything that supports their point of view, and reject that which conflicts with their viewpoints, beliefs, and prior knowledge.

Be aware that, although you may know yourself to be right and you may have all the facts and logical arguments to prove yourself correct and you deliver them in your most persuasive fashion and you *still* may have a prospect who is unmoved by your excellent arguments.

Is there a way to persuade your prospects that your product is good for them, while leaving their current belief system intact? The goal is not to be right; it's to make sales to qualified prospects who can genuinely benefit from what you are selling.

Teleselling Mistake 10: Getting Defensive

No one enjoys rejection. And tellers get it every day—some every hour.

When you are rejected, do not get angry or defensive. The prospect is not rejecting you personally. She is not saying you are bad or inferior or a failure. She is simply indicating that your offer is not right for her, at least not at this time. A "no" doesn't mean you failed. A "no" doesn't mean "no, never." A "no" simply means "no, not now"—nothing more.

Prospects do things for their reasons, not yours. Put yourself in your prospect's shoes. Imagine getting a sales call in the middle of an important meeting . . . or when you just got a delinquency notice from the IRS . . . or when your most important customer just switched to a new vendor. Now can you see why everyone is not thrilled to hear from you, every time you call?

Remember the stockbroker who said my idea of seeing whether his recommended stocks went up before I bought from him was stupid? Earlier, when I told him I was happy with my current brokers, he began to insult them and tell me what losers they were compared to his firm. Even if true, it comes across as whining, and is pitiful rather than impressive.

Teleselling Mistake 11: Being Arrogant

Some marketers deliberately take an ego-based approach. It goes something like this: "I'm wonderful, my product is the best, and if we do business together, it is to your benefit, not mine."

Expect to get rejected when you take this approach. And expect the rejection to be strong. People don't like braggarts. Some people will be impressed and buy when you use the ego-based approach, but many others will be turned off immediately and powerfully.

I prefer the humble approach. Not "I'm the best" or "Our product is the best." But "How can we help you?" . . . "What problems do you have that you think our service might be able to solve for you?" . . . and "Are we the right supplier for you? Let's take a look at your requirements and our products and services, and see if there's a good fit."

When you take the humble approach, you eliminate the risk of offending potential buyers with your ego and pomposity. You also avoid sounding desperate or needy.

With humility comes a sense of power, of control, of being in a service mode rather than a selling mode. Prospects find this attractive. It's almost magnetic. Soft sell . . . don't push too hard . . . and they'll come to you.

I saw a nice example of this in a promotional brochure for Somers White, the financial speaker and consultant. In the brochure, which was written in question-and-answer format, the first question was "Why should I hire Somers White?" The answering text began with this one-sentence paragraph: "Perhaps you should not." It immediately established White as a vendor who does not need the business and only wants to work with customers he can really help.

Pull back. Don't be overeager. If you push hard, people will sense that you want to make a sale, and can manipulate you accordingly. They treat you much better if they perceive there's a chance they can't get you, that you are screening and evaluating *them* as much as they are screening and evaluating you.

Paul Karasik, an independent sales trainer in Weehawken, New Jersey, teaches a closing technique based on the principle that people want what they can't have. He calls it the "take-away close."

When the prospects are resistant or negative, instead of fighting with them, agree with them. And take it a step further by saying, "You're right—perhaps this product isn't really right for you."

When the tables are turned, and it's *you* threatening (in a polite way) not to complete the transaction, the prospects' attitude can change in a hurry. "Whoa, wait a minute," many have said when I've used this close. "Don't be so hasty. I didn't say we weren't interested. There's just a couple of things we want to clarify with you first. . . ." The prospect continues the conversation as an interested potential buyer, eliminating the difficult "show-me" attitude he had expressed prior to the take-away close.

Caution: The take-away close entails risk, because, as you may have guessed, the prospect might agree with your assertion that the product is not right for him, and end the call. Use it only when you are at the stage where you feel the conversation must get back on a positive track, with you in control, or else it's not worth continuing.

TELESELLING MISTAKE 12: NOT HAVING A RESPONSE TO THE PROSPECT'S OBJECTION OR TURN-DOWN OF YOUR OFFER

There are few things as awkward or embarrassing for the teleseller as not knowing what to say.

When a prospect voices an objection or turns you down, immediately launch into a prepared, tested response. Do it coolly, confidently, without being argumentative or adversarial. This is your only chance to keep the sale alive.

Sometimes you won't know what to say. If that's the case, immediately say, "I don't know the answer to that, but let me research it and get back to you." Then set an appointment for a callback to answer the question or objection, preferably within 24 to 48 hours.

How do you learn the right things to say? From experience. After a hundred calls, you'll have a pretty good idea of what prospects are likely to say: common objections, frequent complaints, typical questions. After another couple of hundred calls, you'll have come up with answers to these stock questions and objections, which you can then pull from notes, call guidelines, scripts, memory, or your computer files as the need arises.

Teleselling Mistake 13: Not Bothering to Uncover the Prospect's Real Needs by Asking Questions

Too many tellers do what I call "out-of-context selling." This means they present the features and benefits of their product without first bothering to determine what the prospect needs and wants.

Advertising 101 teaches that prospects buy benefits, not features. Strictly speaking, they buy products that solve a problem or fill a need they have. To sell effectively, you must link the features and benefits of your product to the prospects' problems and needs they satisfy. And to do that, you must know what your prospects' problems and needs are, and which are most important, second most important, and so on down the line.

How do you find this out? By asking questions, of course. The fundamentals of uncovering prospect needs and desires are described in chapters 6 (page 80) and 7 (page 87).

Often prospects will ask, "Why should I buy from you?" The best response I have found is, "I don't know. What do you need?" I listen to their needs. Then, if there is a good fit between my product or service and their need, I structure my presentation accordingly.

If the customer has called you in response to a promotion, or you are having your second or third conversation, and "Why should I buy from you?" comes up, an effective reply is: "Well, you already have a supplier. Yet you're still talking to me. Why?" Of course, the current supplier is not 100 percent satisfactory; otherwise they probably would *not* be talking to you. This response brings that dissatisfaction to the forefront so you can focus on the fact that your product or service does not have the same fault.

Here are some other good questions that can help you uncover prospects' needs, wants, and desires:

- "What are you looking for?"
- "What's the most important factor you'll consider when evaluating this purchasing decision?"
- "What's the biggest problem you're dealing with right now that this type of service might be able to help you with?"
- "If my product were a magic wand and I could wave it to make a miracle happen for you, what would that miracle be?"
- "What are the three most important criteria you will use in evaluating this type of product or service?"

TELESELLING MISTAKE 14: NOT HAVING A RANGE OF OTHER OPTIONS TO OFFER PROSPECTS WHO TURN DOWN YOUR PRIMARY OFFER

Telesellers who offer a broad product line have an advantage over those with a single product sold at a single, fixed, nonnegotiable price.

If you offer or push only one product and the prospect says no, your only option is to get into an argument with her about why she is making a mistake and should in fact purchase the product you are selling. This is an argument you will usually lose.

Having a broad product line gives you flexibility. If one product does not precisely fit the prospect's requirements, you can offer one or more of the others as alternatives. If the price is beyond the prospect's budget, you can offer a scaled-down model that does essentially what the prospect needs but costs less.

If you do not have multiple products or services in your line, consider expanding. Create a broader menu selection enabling prospects to select the item that fits their needs best. The better you meet the prospects' requirements and budget, the more likely you are to close the sale.

TELESELLING MISTAKE 15: REFUSING TO MAIL OR FAX LITERATURE TO REAL PROSPECTS WITH GENUINE INFORMATION WHO ASK TO SEE SOMETHING IN WRITING

A number of sales trainers are "antiliterature," that is, they discourage the sending of sales literature and instead urge you to push the prospect for a telephone or face-to-face appointment. They believe that sending literature is a waste of time, because people just file or trash it without reading it, and the sale stalls as a result. They teach that a request for literature is a stall used by prospects to get you off the phone and avoid getting a sales pitch.

My feeling is they are partially right, but mostly wrong, and their antiliterature approach does more harm than good.

Yes, some prospects may say, "Send me something in the mail" just to get rid of you. But let's look at the flip side:

• Many people, like me, are print-oriented. Even if we don't read it all, we need to have a brochure or other printed literature to which we can refer while speaking to a salesperson. The printed literature also assures us that you are a "real" company and not some fly-by-night operator in a boiler room with a telephone.

• Most buying decisions today are made by a committee of two or more people. Yet you may not speak to them all. The prospect needs something to pass on to other members of the buying committee so he or she can back up a recommendation to buy your items.

• According to a study by Thomas Publishing, 90 percent of industrial purchasing agents said they must have at least one piece of literature from a particular vendor in their files before they will place an order. Therefore, if you sell to businesses and refuse to send literature, you risk losing up to nine out of ten sales.

• Many people's response to an initial sales call is, "Send me some literature." It is a perfectly reasonable request. Therefore, to respond by saying, in essence, "No, we don't want to," arouses suspicion, is off-putting, and ineffective.

Recently a stockbroker called to sell me stock. I had never heard of his firm and said I was interested, but he needed to fax me his company brochure along with an analyst's report on the stock. When he began his standard lecture on why he couldn't do that (the basic argument being that people who request literature are not buyers and therefore sending it is a waste of time), I interrupted and said, "You're right. I can't guarantee that if you send your information, I'll buy, and so in that way it may be a waste of time and effort. But I do not make investments unless I have printed information in hand about the brokerage in general and the stock in particular. If you do not send it, I will pass on this offer."

He hemmed and hawed, thought about it, and faxed what I asked for. Two days later he had a new client and my check for

$10,000. There are many prospects out there who want, like, and need printed information before they'll buy from you. Refuse to send it, play games, or make it difficult to get, and they will buy elsewhere. This is a fact.

• When you follow up, the prospect or her assistant may try to put you off with "Send me something." If you've already sent it, and they received it, this stall won't work anymore. The prospect either has to tell you she's not interested or agree to talk with you, since there's nothing else to mail. So sending literature avoids this as a sales block later on.

• Many sales trainers warn that all prospects ever do with literature is file it. That's not true. But even when prospects do file your brochure, you may benefit: Later on, when they have a need for that type of product, they'll look in their reference folder and find your material with your phone number on it. I've gotten tens of thousands of dollars' worth of consulting and copywriting assignments from people who had received my literature, filed it, and were calling me 6, 12, even 18 months to 2 years later.

Many people need you later, not now. Many people keep reference files of catalogs, brochures, and other vendor literature. Not to accommodate them is foolish.

The bottom line: If a prospect asks for more information, send it. If the information is for file reference or a nonurgent need, mail it. If the prospect is hot, e-mail or fax your literature within an hour or two after you promise to do so. In our office we ask the prospect, "How do you want this sent—mail, FedEx, fax, or e-mail?"

Then follow up to make sure it was received, answer any questions, and find out what the next step is in the buying process. If the prospect doesn't suggest a specific action, say to him or her,

"You have our material. What do you want to happen next?" This will help move you along to the next logical step.

Teleselling Mistake 16: Forgetting to Ask for Referrals from Prospects Who Turn You Down

When most people are rejected by anyone, for anything—a sale, a proposal, a job interview, a recommendation—they say, "Thank you" curtly and end the conversation.

That's a mistake. Even if a prospect turns you down, you should always ask for referrals, just as you should from a customer. Ask as follows:

"I appreciate your time today, Mr. X. I understand you're not interested. But may I ask you a question? Do you have colleagues at other companies—not competing with yours, of course—that might be interested in my product?"

When the prospect gives you a name and phone number, you say, "Thank you" and ask for two or three more.

You will get a better response calling referred leads than names on a cold list. That's because you are referencing a familiar name, someone the prospect already knows.

By asking for referrals on every "no," you get more referrals, more of your telephone calls are to referral leads, and you get a better result than if most of your calls are to total strangers. Try it. It works.

Teleselling Mistake 17: Not Qualifying Prospects Up Front

Has this ever happened to you? You call a prospect, get her attention, present your product, and answer her questions. You send literature and more literature. You play telephone tag, leave voice-mail messages, have brief conversations. Finally, the prospect is ready to order. "Great," you say. "That will be one hundred fifty dollars for a ten-gallon drum." "What!" complains the prospect. "We can get it for one hundred twenty dollars down the street." She quickly hangs up. You don't make the sale. And all that time is wasted.

Or: You call a prospect to sell her your product. She is interested. You make your presentation, prepare a cost estimate, send it out, and hear nothing. When you call back she tells you, "Oh, I think it would be great, but my husband says he can do it himself." Again, your time is wasted.

What happened? In both situations, you didn't qualify the prospect early enough in the selling process. In the first case, you didn't find out the budget before presenting the price (or at least give an indication of your cost structure before forging ahead with your presentation and follow-up effort). In the second case, you assumed the woman would make a decision on her own, then found out later she was not willing to do this.

Before going very far with prospects, it is important to qualify them. You want to know:

- Are you talking to the right person (the decision maker)?
- Is this person the sole decision maker or must you expand your sales effort to include others on the buying committee?
- Does the company have a budget? Can they afford your product or service?
- Is there a fit? Does the prospect have a need for the product or service you are selling, or a problem that your product or service can solve?

You learn from experience—and from instinct and feeling—when to qualify the prospect. The earlier you can qualify your prospects, the less time you'll waste selling to prospects who cannot or will not buy. See the scripts and guidelines in chapters 6 and 7 for steps you can take to qualify prospects before you try to sell them something.

Parting thoughts

Recently I gave an attorney who wanted to market a particular product a checklist of ways he could possibly generate sales. It contained many of the things he expected, including newspaper ads, direct mailings, and Yellow Pages ads. But when he saw that teleselling was on the list, he almost couldn't believe it.

"I hate telephone sales calls," he said, "I don't like to make them, and I don't like to get them. Why is it on our list of things to test?"

The answer is that in marketing you never know what will work unless you test it. Your preconceived notions of what will and won't get results for your product or service are just that—notions. They are not fact.

"The only way an argument in advertising and marketing can be settled is by running a test," said the ad agency giant Claude Hopkins. "Not by arguments and discussions held sitting around a conference table."

It's the same for any marketing and selling tool, including telephone selling. Will it work for you? You won't know until you test it. And remember, testing telephone sales campaigns is easy. You have everything to gain—especially if it works—and very little to lose.

Some of you came to this book as practitioners of telephone selling, hoping to learn a few techniques for doing it even better. I hope I've lived up to your expectations.

Others were skeptics. You instinctively feel teleselling is ineffective or inappropriate for your industry, product, or marketplace.

But at the same time, you see that traditional methods alone aren't doing the job.

In that case, I have a favor to ask. Give telephone selling a try. Test it. If it doesn't work, test it some more. The great thing about teleselling is that you can do some rather extensive testing for less than what you'd pay for even a small ad in the Yellow Pages or an insert in just one issue of the Sunday paper.

As for the results you will get, who knows? Perhaps you'll enjoy it more than you think. And your customers will respond to it better than you expected. Increased sales and profits await those who experiment in this domain of "dialing for dollars." Why not give it a whirl? Best of luck! And please let me know how it turns out.

Index

absenteeism, office, 41
accessibility, 160–61
accounting, 10
add-on sales, 178–86
    referrals, 178–80
    repeat business and reorders, 180–83
    upgrading, 182–84
    upselling, 184–86
advantages to teleselling, 5–12
advertising, 3, 7, 14, 17, 209
    costs, 9
    follow-up calls, 12
    print, 3, 6, 7, 204–7
    timing, 11
    Yellow Pages, 3, 17, 18, 26, 209, 210
aggression, 13, 154, 190
American Productivity and Quality Center, 174
anger, 195, 199
annoyance, 195
answer/ask strategy, 114–16, 118
answering machines, 49, 50, 161
answers, lack of, 201–2
antiliterature approach, 204–7
apples-to-oranges comparison, 103
appointment books, 136

arguing with prospects, 195–98, 203–4
arrogance, 199–201
Art of Self-Promotion, The, 128
AT&T phones, 43
AT&T Wireless Services, 49
attendee lists, 63–64
attitude, 21, 32–36, 161
authentication, 48
average size of order, 70
average unit of sale, 56, 59

bad time, catching customers at a, 188–90
Barnes, Roscoe III, *Discover Your Talent and Find Fulfillment*, 36
beating deadlines, 170–71
benefit/advantage teleselling, 86–87
benefit statement script, 78–80
Benun, Ilise, 128, 143
Better Business Bureau, 16
Bishop, Bill, 113–17
"boss/committee/spouse has to approve" objection, 109–10
broad product line, 203–4
brochures, refusal to send, 204–7
brokers, list, 65, 66, 68–72, 73
budget, 101, 106–7, 169–70

Index

Business Breakthroughs, 149
business factors, 68
buyer's market, 2
buying cycles and patterns, 35, 39, 67–68

calendars, 136
Cali, John M., Jr., 174
callbacks, 116–18, 133
Call Center, 10–11
caller ID, 16, 23, 44, 50
call forwarding, 23, 44, 46–47
call guidelines, *see* scripts
calling at off-hours, 113–14, 119
calling list, *see* list, calling
calls per day required, 56, 58–59, 60
call transfer, 46
call volume, 56, 57–58, 59, 61
call waiting, 23, 44, 47
canned opening, of script, 190–92
catalogue sales, 4, 7, 63, 64, 67, 70, 184
catching customers at a bad time, 188–90
cellular phones, 47–49
    features, 47–49
Cellular Telecommunications Industry
    Association (CTIA), 47
center, teleselling, *see* selling center
chair, 43, 51
Chamber of Commerce, 74
charging less than the estimate, 169–70
cheaper-is-not-better tactic, 107–109
Cidco, 43
closing the sale, 142–54
    avoiding time-limited offers and pres-
        sure sales, 148–50
    being comfortable with, 153–54
    confidence in, 147–48
    constant, 151
    prospect's help in, 151–53
    techniques, 144–48
    "what do you want to happen next?"
        approach, 143
clothing, 23–24
cold calls, 76–112
    objection script, 97–112
    opening script, 76–84
    presentation script, 85–96
    tips, 83–84

cold prospects, follow-up calls for, 123
commercials, TV, 17
"committee/boss/spouse has to approve"
    objection, 109–10
common sense, 21
common telephone selling mistakes,
    187–209
company name, 51–52, 78–79
compensation for customer trouble,
    163–64
competition, 2, 156
    differentiation from, 175–76
compiled lists, 63
computers, 9, 26, 40, 51, 181
    contact-management programs, 132,
        137–39, 172
    follow-up on, 137–39
    Internet, 3–4, 7, 10, 17, 44, 53, 103
    leased, 43
    modem, 44, 45
    repair, 184–85
    software, 10–11, 21, 22, 43, 132, 137–39,
        172, 182
    telephone systems, 23
    upgrades, 182, 183
conference calling, 45
confidence, 147–48
Consumer Reports, 49
contact-management software, 132, 137–39,
    172
contracts, 35, 36
controlled-circulation lists, 64
conventional sales, decline of, 1–5
conversion rate, 55, 56–57, 59, 60, 61
corporate downsizing, 3
cost of ownership vs. cost of purchase,
    101–2
cost reductions, 169–70
costs, teleselling, 9–10
credit, 163–64
credit cards, 8, 186
    holder lists, 64–65
customer service, 2, 5, 30, 44, 155–77, 186
    creating realistic expectations, 156–58
    delivering more than promised, 158–73
    differentiation from competition,
        175–76

diligence in offering, 173–75
   listening, 176–77
   upgrade calls, 183
cycles, buying, 35, 39, 67–68

Davis, Paul D., 145
deadlines, 157–58
   beating, 170–71
dedication, 18
defensiveness, 199
delivery, 156–57, 186
demographics, 67
demoralization of teleselling, 13–15
desk, 22, 43
determination, 36–39
dialogue/back-and-forth teleselling, 92–93
differentiator, 104–5
diligence, 173–75
direct mail, 3, 6, 7, 8, 14, 25, 26, 28, 54, 72, 73, 74, 148
   costs, 9, 10
   follow-up calls, 12
Direct Marketing, 68
directories, 72–75
   industry, 63, 72–75
   prospecting, 72–75
Directories in Print, 74
direct-sales approach, 94–96
disadvantages of teleselling, 13–18
discounts, 12, 163–64, 185
DM NEWS, 68
donor lists, 64
do not disturb, 46
   sign, 23, 42
downsizing, 3
dress, 23–24
dry spells, 37

easy payment plans, 99–101
economy, 1
effectiveness, 5–6
effort, 21–22, 36–39
ego-based approach, 199–201
elements of successful teleselling, 20–39
   attitude, 21, 32–36, 161
   follow-up, 21, 29–30, 121–41
   list, 11, 20, 25–27, 62–75, 84, 178

perseverance, 21–22, 36–39
plan, 20, 24–25, 36, 54–61
scripts, 8, 20–21, 27–29, 30, 62, 76–112
selling center, 20, 22–24, 40–53
skills, 21, 31–32
e-mail, 33, 44, 51, 63, 150, 206
   follow-up, 123
embarrassment, 153–54
empathy, 21
Encyclopedia of Associations, 74
enhanced registration, 48–49
enthusiasm, 32–33
environment, *see* selling center
equipment, 10–11, 22, 40
   answering machine, voice mail, and answering services, 49–50
   leased, 43, 185
   selling center, 43–50
   telephone, 43–50
estimates, 169
   charging less than, 169–70
evasiveness, teleselling, 192–94
exceeding sales quotas, 178–86
experience, 202
extra function keys, 45
extra-length phone cord, 45
extra product or service, 167–69

face-to-face sales, 12
Farber, Barry J., 106
fast action, 150
fax, 8, 30, 44, 45, 52–53, 63, 119, 122, 150, 169
   on demand, 52–53
   follow-up, 123, 135–36
   refusing to fax literature to prospects, 204–7
fear, 38, 153–54
Federal Express, 42, 150, 206
fee reductions, 163–64
fighting with prospects, 197–98
files, 21, 51, 136
   organized, 171–72
   paper, 136–37
financial services, 13, 181, 197, 199, 205
financing, 99–101, 185–86
flexibility, 15, 28

Index

focus groups, 68
follow-up, 21, 29–30, 121–41, 186
  computerized, 137–39
  fast response, 122
  getting unanswered calls retrieved, 135–36
  keeping track of prospects, 136–39
  measuring results, 128–29
  prospects for, 126–28
  scripts for typical situations, 130–35
  strategies that work, 122–24
  timing, 129–30
  unanswered calls, 135–36, 139–41
  understanding prospect response, 124–26
  unexpected, 164–65
free gifts, 159–60
"free seconds" approach, 167–69

Geller, Lois, 174
gender, 67
geography, 66
getting past the secretary, 113–20
gifts, 180
  free, 159–60
Gilbert, Dr. Rob, 38
goal, sales, 60
guarantees, 110–11

hang-up calls, 33
Hardy, Jerry, 155
headsets, 22, 40–41, 45
health care, 198
"hold" button, 45
Hopkins, Claude, 209
"hotlines," list, 68, 70
house list, 63
humility, 200

IBM, 5
immediate response, 8–9
income objective, 55, 56, 59
incremental closes, 145–47
index cards, 136
individual communication, xv
industry directories, 63, 72–75
in-house lists, 65

interaction, telephone, 7–8
International Thomson Retail Press (ITRP), 65
Internet, 3–4, 7, 10, 17, 44, 53, 103
interruptions, 42
invoice, under estimate, 169–70
irritation, 195
ISDN compatibility, 44

journals, trade, 74

Karasik, Paul, 5, 37, 200–201
keeping track of prospects, 136–39
Kipen Publishing Corporation, 5

leased equipment, 43, 185
LeasePower 5, 137
leasing plans, 99–101
LED display, 44
letters, 30
  follow-up, 123, 124
library, 74
list, calling, 11, 20, 25–27, 62–75, 84, 178
  active vs. inactive and buyer vs. prospect, 70
  availability, 11, 17
  average size of order, 70
  brokers, 65, 66, 68–72, 73
  cost per thousand, 69–70
  description, 70
  evaluating list recommendations, 69–71
  importance of, 25–27
  managers, 65–66, 71, 72
  market research as aid to, 68
  ordering, 71–72
  owners, 65, 72
  profiling your target market, 66–68
  selections available, 71
  size, 69
  sources, 75
  types of, 63–65, 70
  updating, 71, 73
  usage report, 70–71
  vendors, 65–66
listening, 88–89, 151–52, 176–77, 194
literature, refusing to fax or mail, 204–7
lodging, 9

loyalty, customer, 2, 174–75
lunch, 84

mailed literature, 204–7
mail-order offers, 63, 64, 67, 70, 184
major closes, 145
managers, list, 65–66, 71, 72
marketing, conventional, 1–5
market research, 68
mass communication, xv
Master Prospector, 114
measuring results, 128–29
membership lists, 63–64
memory dial, 44
merged database lists, 65
message waiting indicator, 46
mistakes, teleselling, 187–209
  arguing or fighting with prospects,
    195–98, 203–4
  arrogance, 199–201
  catching customers at a bad time,
    188–90
  evasiveness, 192–94
  forgetting to use referrals, 207
  not asking permission to give sales pitch,
    190–92
  not changing tone in response to
    prospect's reactions, 195
  not knowing what to say, 201–2
  not qualifying prospects up-front, 207–9
  out-of-context selling, 202–3
  refusing to mail or fax literature, 204–7
  script-reading, 194–95
  single product line, 203–4
  telling prospects they are stupid, 196–97
  trying to prove you are right, 198–99
mobile phones, *see* cellular phones
modem, 44, 45
Moshman, Bob, *Home Incorporated*, 51
multiple phone lines, 44–45

name:
  company, 51–52, 78–79
  of secretary, 133
needs, prospect's, 202–3
  prospect need-qualification script, 80–82,
    191, 192, 193

negativity, 132–33, 201
neutrality, 131–32
New England Medical Journal, 198
new marketplace, difficulties of, 1–2
new products/offers, 12
Northern Telecom, 43
notepads, 22, 23
notes, *see* scripts

objection/answer scenarios, 111–12
objections, telling prospects their, 196–
    97
objection script, 97–112
  "my boss/committee/spouse has to
    approve" objection, 109–10
  overcoming price objections, 98–109
  practice objection/answer scenarios,
    111–12
  satisfaction pledge, 110–11
off-hours, calling at, 113–14, 119
office, 22–24, 40–53
  absenteeism, 41
opening script, 76–84
  benefit statement script, 78–80
  prospect need-qualification script,
    80–82, 191, 192, 193
  shift delivery to accommodate prospect
    mood, 82–83
organized files, 171–72
out-of-context selling, 202–3
overpromising, 156
owners, list, 65, 72

pagers, 48, 161
paid-circulation lists, 64
paper files, 136–37
paper glut, 7
Para Publishing, 52–53
patterns and cycles, buying, 35, 39, 67–68
Paston, Ken, 97
performance promise, 110–11
perseverance, 21–22, 36–39
personal attention, 165–66
personal information managers, 138
Peters, Tom, *In Search of Excellence*, 175,
    198
phone cord, extra-length, 45

Index

plan, teleselling, 20, 24–25, 36, 54–61
 average unit of sale and sales volume,
  55, 59
 calls per day required, 56, 58–59, 60
 call volume and prospecting rate, 56,
  57–58, 59, 60, 61
 conversion rate, 55, 56–57, 59, 60, 61
 income objective, 55, 56, 59
 summary of, 59–60
politeness, 161–63
positive attitude, 32–36, 161
postage, 4
postcard, 30
practice, 31–32, 84, 194
 objection/answer scenarios, 111–12
preference sell, 95
presentation script, 85–96
 benefit/advantage, 86–87
 dialogue/back-and-forth, 92–93
 direct-sales approach, 94–96
 survey/question, 87–92
pressure selling, 148–50
prestige, lack of, 16–17
price objections, overcoming, 98–109
prima donna vendors, 172–73
print advertising, 3, 4, 6, 7, 204–7
privacy, 41
problem correction and compensation,
  162–64
production rate, 17, 54–55
profits, 39
 increasing with teleselling, 1–19
promises:
 overpromising, 156
 underpromising, 156–58
promotions, xv, 12
promptness, 161–63
prospect calls, timing of, 113–14
prospecting directories, 72–75
prospecting rate, 56, 57–58, 60, 61
prospect need-qualification script, 80–82,
  191, 192, 193
prospect's permission for sales pitch,
  190–92
proving you are right, 198–99
psychographics, 67
push-button dialing, 44, 83

qualified leads, follow-up calls for, 123
qualifying prospects, 207–9
quotas, exceeding sales, 178–86

Radio Shack, 49
rapport building, 92–93
realistic expectations, creating, 156–58
receptionists, see secretaries and receptionists
redial, 45
reference materials, 74
referrals, 178–80, 207
rejection, 13–15, 37, 55, 84, 134, 135, 153,
  154, 199, 200, 207
repeat business and reorders, 151, 155, 163,
  178, 180–83
resellers, 137
response lists, 63
response rates, 6–7, 25, 37, 38
risk removal, 149–50
Roman (Edith) Associates, 26
room temperature, 23, 50
rudeness, 15–16

sales, add-on, see add-on sales
Sales Consultants International, 7
sales database programs, 138
sales pitch, asking permission to give,
  190–92
sales quotas, exceeding, 178–86
sales volume, 56, 59
satisfaction pledge, 110–11
scaled-back offer, 104
scripts, 8, 20–21, 27–29, 30, 62, 76–112
 benefit statement, 78–80
 canned opening, 190–92
 follow-up, 130–35
 objection, 97–112
 opening, 76–84
 presentation, 85–96
 prospect need-qualification, 80–82, 191,
  192, 193
 sounding natural, 194–95
secretaries and receptionists, 8, 113–20,
  133, 176, 193
 answer/ask strategy, 114–16, 118
 blocked by, 133

call-backs, 116–18, 133
  getting past, 113–20, 133
  name of, 133
  timing of prospect calls, 113–14
  treating them right, 118–19
selective call acceptance, 46
self-employment, 16, 18
selling center, 20, 22–24, 40–53
  company name, 51–52
  equipment, 43–50
  fax on demand, 52–53
  telephone, 43–50
  well-designed, 42–43
  work space, 50–51
Selling magazine, 5, 7
seminar lists, 63–64
seminars, 11, 12
service contracts, 184, 185
short-message service (SMS), 48
single-number reach, 46
single product line, 203–4
skills, 21, 31–32
sleep mode, 47–48
Small Business Computing, 106
smiling, 24
software, computer, 10–11, 21, 22, 43, 132,
    172, 182
  contact-management, 132, 137–39, 172
solitude, 41
speaker phones, 22, 45
speaking voice, *see* voice
special offers, 12, 166–67, 186
"spouse/boss/committee has to approve"
    objection, 109–10
Starting Smart, 5
"sticker shock," 98–99
subscription lists, 64
success, elements of, 20–39
survey/question teleselling, 87–92
surveys, 12

take-away close, 200–201
target market, profiling, 66–68
Target Marketing, 68, 174
telemarketing, xv, 6, 54, 62
telephone, 43–50, 83

cellular, 47–49
  features, 43–47
telephone answering services, 49–50
teleselling, xv
  advantages of, 5–12
  common mistakes, 187–209
  definition of, xv
  disadvantages of, 13–18
  elements of, 20–39
terminal, 40
terminology, xv
thank-you notes, 180
three-way calling, 44, 45
time commitment, 10
Time-Life Books, 155
time-limited offers, 148–50
timing, 34
  bad, to reach prospects, 188–90
  follow-up, 129–30
  promptness, 161–63
  of prospect calls, 113–14
titles, 51–52, 79–80
Toastmasters, 195
tone, changes in, 195
touch tone, 44, 83
trade journals, 74
trade shows, 3, 9, 11, 12, 64
traditional sales, decline of, 1–5
Trahey, Jane, 38
training seminars, 32
travel, 4, 9
TV commercials, 17
two-tier pricing, 149

unanswered calls, 122
  getting them returned, 135–36, 139–41
underpromising, 156–58
unexpected follow-up, 164–65
upgrading, 178, 182–84
UPS, 42
upselling, 178, 184–86

vacation, 2
vagueness, 192–94
value-conscious buyers, 105–6
Vaughn, Paul, 169
vendors, list, 65–66

Index

voice, 21, 83–84, 194
changes in tone, 195
voice-activated dialing, 45–46
voice mail, 9, 23, 44, 45, 46, 49–50, 119–20, 161, 176
message retrieval, 46
partial message, 119–20

Warde, Robert, 5
warranties, 110–11, 184, 185, 186
Weinstein, Anne, 83

Weiss, Fred, 97
White, Somers, 200
Williams, A.L., *All You Can Do Is All You Can Do*, 175–76
Wood, David, 122
Woodall, Bob, 7
work space, *see* selling center
World Wide Web, 3–4

Yellow Pages, 3, 17, 18, 26, 63, 68, 209, 210

About the Author

Bob Bly is the director of the Center for Technical Communication, a consulting firm that helps businesspeople improve their communications skills. CTC presents seminars and training sessions to association and corporate clients nationwide on sales, marketing, writing, customer service, and related business communication topics.

Bly is the author of more than thirty books, including *The Elements of Business Writing* (Macmillan), *How to Promote Your Own Business* (NAL), *The Copywriter's Handbook* (Henry Holt), and *Selling Your Services* (Henry Holt). Other titles include *Creative Careers* (John Wiley), *Business to Business Direct Marketing* (NTC), and *Keeping Clients Satisfied* (Prentice Hall).

Bob Bly's articles have appeared in such publications as *Computer Decisions*, *Writer's Digest*, *Amtrak Express*, *Cosmopolitan*, *Science Books & Films*, *Chemical Engineering*, *New Jersey Monthly*, *Business Marketing*, and *Direct*. Organizations that have hired the author as a trainer and speaker include the Cincinnati Direct Marketing Association, Thoroughbred Software Leaders' Conference, Walker Richer & Quinn, ARCO Chemical, International Tile Expositions, Learning Annex, Creative Group, Cardiac Pacemakers Inc., the U.S. Army, Dow Chemical,

About the Author

Mail Order Association of Nurseries, Foxboro, IBM, McGraw-Hill, and the International Laboratory Distributors Association.

Questions and comments on *Secrets of Successful Telephone Selling* may be sent to:

Bob Bly
Center for Technical Communication
22 East Quackenbush Avenue
Dumont, N.J. 07628
Tel: 201-385-1220
Fax: 201-385-1138
e-mail: Rwbly@aol.com